The
Red
Azalea

The
Red
Azalea

Chinese Poetry
since the
Cultural Revolution

EDITED BY
EDWARD MORIN

TRANSLATED BY
FANG DAI, DENNIS DING, AND EDWARD MORIN

INTRODUCTION BY
LEO OU-FAN LEE

UNIVERSITY OF HAWAII PRESS
HONOLULU

LIBRARY OF CONGRESS CATALOGING-IN-PUBLICATION DATA

THE RED AZALEA : CHINESE POETRY SINCE THE
CULTURAL REVOLUTION / EDITED BY EDWARD MORIN ;
TRANSLATED BY FANG DAI, DENNIS DING, AND EDWARD
MORIN ; INTRODUCTION BY LEO OU-FAN LEE.
        P.   CM.
    INCLUDES BIBLIOGRAPHICAL REFERENCES.
    ISBN 0-8248-1256-5 (ALK. PAPER). — ISBN
0-8248-1320-0 (PBK. : ALK. PAPER)
    I. CHINESE POETRY—20TH CENTURY—TRANSLATIONS
INTO ENGLISH.   2. ENGLISH POETRY—TRANSLATIONS
FROM CHINESE.   I. MORIN, EDWARD, 1934-   . II.
DAI, FANG, 1955-   . III. DING, DENNIS, 1942-   .
PL2658.E3R33   1990
895.1'15208—DC20   90-41829
                                                   CIP

UNIVERSITY OF HAWAII PRESS BOOKS ARE PRINTED
ON ACID-FREE PAPER AND MEET THE GUIDELINES
FOR PERMANENCE AND DURABILITY OF THE COUNCIL
ON LIBRARY RESOURCES

CONTENTS

PREFACE

A T our first meeting in early 1986, Dennis Ding told me about the young "obscurist poets" of Beijing who had reintroduced personal feeling, ambiguity, and stylistic innovation into Chinese poetry after the decade of barbarism called the Cultural Revolution. Their officially unsanctioned magazine *Today* created groundswell changes in public taste which more recent repression has not yet fully eradicated. I asked to see some of the new poetry, and within a week Dennis made literal translations of short poems by Shu Ting and Gu Cheng. Discussing the poems line by line, we worked toward polished English versions and turned next to Xu Gang's "Red Azalea on the Cliff," which epitomizes the frustration and alienation expressed by many poets after the Cultural Revolution.

During that ordeal, when many Chinese translations of foreign books were banned or destroyed, Dennis was in college. His mother complained that she had nothing to read, so after daytime classes Dennis stayed up late surreptitiously translating an English-language edition of Flaubert's *Madame Bovary* into Chinese. As he progressed into the story of Emma Bovary's discontent, Dennis grew more in touch with his own; yet, in the interest of personal and social survival, he had to abandon the translation project at midpoint in the novel.

In December 1986, when I met Fang Dai at a bilingual reading, he and a colleague remarked that, although Dennis and I had inevitably lost some of the multiple connotations in certain Chinese expressions, we had also turned some Chinese clichés into fresh, idiomatic English. Making this a three-way collaboration, Fang has greatly enhanced the accuracy and nuances of these translations; our association over three years has been an education for me in recent cultural and literary developments. Finally, Professor Leo Ou-fan Lee, a foremost authority on twentieth-century Chinese literature, has provided an invaluable introduction which traces the lineage and continuity of the new poetry within the historical framework of Chinese modernism beginning with the May Fourth Movement.

My co-translators and I have chosen poems for this anthology on the basis of their literary merit rather than for timely or documentary interest. Although we selected no poem for topical or political attributes, we have nevertheless included some personal poems with socio-political implications. The familiar distinction American poets often make between personal and political discourse seems hardly applicable to writing in China, where governmental presence is so pervasive that even the most private statements can have serious public consequences. Yet this anthology excludes the kind of political poetry which was fashionable during the Cultural Revolution. Unlike American political poetry with its tendency to protest against the establishment, much political poetry in China has served the pragmatic ends of a current regime, helping to establish its legitimacy and improve public morale by criticizing a previous regime or Western capitalism. Even though some of the poems we have translated do speak disdainfully of living conditions during the Cultural Revolution, they refrain from optimistic praise of the current regime. These are not political poems in the Chinese sense of the term.

As Eastern European writers have shown, poetry can sometimes be a more reliable witness than journalism. Several of the poets included in this book observe the convention of writing the date of composition after the text of a poem—a counterpart of the convention in Chinese classical poetry of using the place and date of composition in, or even as, a poem's title. A date standing alone after a contemporary poem always means date of composition, not publication. Besides informing readers where the work fits into the chronology of a poet's work, a composition date documents the historical context and its accompanying social conditions. In a nation of abruptly changing policies, this convention can be artistically relevant to understanding the emotions expressed in a poem. In Bei Dao's "Rainy Night," for instance, the speaker may appear histrionic, perhaps sentimental, until we realize that in 1976—the last year of the Cultural Revolution—the writing and publication of a candid personal poem could have brought severe official sanctions upon the author.

For readers of Chinese, we have included the original texts of one or two poems by each author in a section at the back of the book. We have also made every effort to find the place and date of first publication for all the poems. When available, this information (usually a magazine title) is noted at the bottom of the page—the translated title followed by the *pinyin* romanization in parentheses. If the place of first publication is unknown, the source note cites only the translated title of a subsequent collection from which our translation was made. We have used anthologies and single-author collections extensively as translation sources; the bibliography contains those titles in both English and Chinese.

The poems selected for this anthology have the emotional and technical qualities of literature and can hold their own alongside excellent poetry written elsewhere in the world. The poets represented here are sometimes very direct in expressing personal emotions, an antipathy for opportunism, and a desire to rethink the direction their society is taking. It may be easy to criticize contemporary Chinese poems, as well as these translations, for a lack of the complication or sophistication that modernist readers have come to expect. However, we believe that a large number of poems in this anthology possess those qualities, though not necessarily in ways that Westerners appreciate. The poems have been written for and read by a substantial audience in China that extends far beyond the tribe of poets and other creative writers. Many of these poems may prove permanently valuable because they have something emotionally serious at stake—love, survival, human dignity, the struggle to maintain hope. Finally, the poems transcend a doctrinaire provincialism that once seemed invincible, and in the process achieve a universal human appeal for readers of literature everywhere.

We would like to thank Professors Eugene Eoyang of Indiana University, William Tay of the University of California at San Diego, Perry Link of Princeton University, and Zhou Shizhong and Mu Shampei of Northwest University in Xi'an for their suggestions on translating individual poems. We also thank Göran Malmqvist of the Swedish Academy, Louis Simpson and Leif Sjoberg of SUNY at Stony Brook, Maxine Kumin in New Hampshire, Paul Engle and Hualing Nieh of the University of Iowa, Wai-lim Yip of the University of California at San Diego, Michael S. Duke of the University of

British Columbia, and John Minford of the University of Auckland in New Zealand for their encouragement and advice.

Joan Gartland, Patricia Hooper, Mitzi Alvin, Larry Pike, Kathleen Ripley Leo, Daniel Minock, and others in the Detroit Writers Group made valuable comments on later drafts of the translations. Stuart Kiang, Grace Wiersma, Pamela Kelley, Jean Brady, Stephanie Chun, and others at the University of Hawaii Press worked directly to make this book an elegant production. Jicheng Lin provided valuable assistance with the bibliography.

Some of these translations have appeared in the following publications: *Amicus Journal, Chariton Review, Crosscurrents, Denver Quarterly, Frank: An International Journal of Writing & Art, The Hawaii Review, The Minnesota Review, New Orleans Review, Paintbrush, Ploughshares, Poetry Miscellany, Poetry World, Rackham Journal of the Arts and Humanities (RaJAH), Sandscript, Screens and tasted parallels, The Third World (Pig Iron,* no. 15), *TriQuarterly, University of Windsor Review, Webster Review, Windless Orchard,* and *Men and Women—Together and Alone* (Iowa City, Ia.: The Spirit That Moves Us Press, 1988).

EDWARD MORIN
Ann Arbor, Michigan

INTRODUCTION

THE appearance of this comprehensive anthology of contemporary poetry from the People's Republic of China—perhaps the most comprehensive to date since it includes representative selections from several generations of modern Chinese poets—is an occasion for joy and celebration. As these copious samples show, post-Mao poetry writing in China has reached a stage where both vitality of creative imagination and diversity of individual styles are clearly discernible. After three decades of domination by Maoist ideology, which viewed poetry, like any other genre of literature, as a vehicle or "instrument" to reflect and inculcate a limited range of political objectives set forth by the Party, contemporary Chinese poetry has won a final victory in its struggle to be itself—that is, to be simply literature, free from the forced agenda of politics. We are therefore in a position to appreciate it as art, no longer mere sociopolitical documentation. For most Western readers, of course, the notion of poetry as literature is commonplace, and the battle to return poetry to the realm of art may seem hardly worth the effort. But in China, this effort has been especially difficult because it is burdened with the complex legacy of modern history.

In this introduction, I would like to lay out the general background of modern Chinese poetry against which these selections from more current eras may best be understood.

I

It is commonly acknowledged that modern Chinese poetry was born amid the Literary Revolution of 1917, which ushered in an intellectual revolution known as the May Fourth Movement. As I have written elsewhere (in the introduction to a volume of recent fiction), the most obvious feature of this May Fourth legacy is a preoccupation with China's multitude of pressing political, economic, and cultural problems—concerns reflected not only in the choice of subject matter by modern Chinese writers but also in how and why they wrote. Driven by an acute historical consciousness (some would call it "ideology") and a keen sense of mission, most of these writers saw the main function of imaginative writing to be the truthful depiction of the social reality of the times. They wanted to hasten the destruction of the ancient and decrepit social order so that from its ashes a new China could be created. It is hardly surprising, then, that realism was the dominant school in most of the arts—long before it was given a revolutionary vision and objective in Mao's famous Talks at the Yan'an Forum on Art and Literature in 1942—and later became the official doctrine of socialist realism that was transformed, after the Sino-Soviet split, into the combination of "revolutionary realism" and "revolutionary romanticism."

This ideological lineage, extending from the realism of social conscience to a Party-directed and Maoist-style socialist realism, is evident in the bulk of modern Chinese fiction—both the short story and the novel—from the early 1920s to the outbreak of the Cultural Revolution in 1966. In a sense, the formal capacity of fiction to encompass either a slice of life or a segment of society offers the modern Chinese writer an appropriate medium in which to fulfil his or her moral obligation to society. Whether or not the potential of fiction as a didactic form has been fully realized is another matter. In poetry, however, the situation was more complicated. True, there was a similar penchant for realism in the early vernacular *(baihua)* poetry experiments. Hu Shi, one of the leaders of the Literary Revolution, argued forcefully in favor of employing exclusively a "living" language in poetry that would reflect the living reality of the present. However, despite his efforts to be truly colloquial, he was unable to forsake end rhymes and metrical patterns—a set of formal habits he had inherited from classical Chinese poetry. For instance, his celebrated poem "Butterflies" was written in neat quatrains of five characters per line and differs little from a classical poem except in its conspicuous use of colloquial phrases. What Hu had not fully realized is that a poetic revolution demands a new poetic form and language. He was not fully aware that living speech alone does not constitute a poetic language; poetry, whether classical or modern, must be cast in a form that marks its generic difference from fiction. Many of the poets of the early May Fourth period—Hu Shi, Yu Pingbo, Liu Dabai, and Zhu Ziqing among others—wrote both poetry and prose in *baihua*, and they do not seem to have paid much attention to differences of genre. The result was a spate of poetic works that in fact read like prose: they seem "poetic" only in that each colloquial sentence (or two) begins a new line.

What these early poets wished to convey in their jejune attempts was the "reality" of their sentiment, captured, so they felt, by the freedom and immediacy of their unadorned colloquial style. In this self-fulfilling merger of the author's intention and the work's content, the mediating role of form seems unimportant. But it does not take a sophisticated intelligence to notice the glaring inadequacies of these experimental works, which in fact served to give modern Chinese poetry a "bad start" and a bad name in the eyes of cultural conservatives—examples of an inferior art when compared to the glorious works of ancient poetry in all their splendid variety: *shi, ci,* and *fu*. By the mid–1920s, a number of students returning from Europe and America—Xu Zhimo and Wen Yiduo in particular—were already conscious of this "formalistic crisis." In a famous essay called "The Form of Poetry" (1926), Wen Yiduo considered form to be inevitable in poetry. He compared the poetic act to playing chess: "No game can be played without rules; no poem can be written without form." While Wen explored both auditory and visual patterns in his own poetry, a poetry that emphasizes, according to Julia Lin, "structural symmetry," Xu Zhimo openly argued for the adaptation of English metrical patterns and rhyme schemes.

From hindsight it is apparent that Xu's Western-inspired poetic form proved not so enduring. What he and Wen had achieved, in my view, is a more sophisticated poetic imagery that brings modern Chinese poetry beyond the superficialities of mimesis and confession. In this regard, each of them can be said to have evolved a poetic language that is characterized by original images—images of beauty chiseled from a landscape and given a romantic and exotic hue (Xu) or turned into an allegory for the nation (Wen's famous poem "Dead Water"). But with Xu's untimely death in the plane-crash of 1931 and Wen's turning from poetry writing to scholarship and political activity, their unfinished task was left to be picked up by the slightly younger generation of poets who became active in the early 1930s. Ai Qing, the oldest poet represented in the present anthology, belongs to this "younger" generation. One can argue that modern Chinese poetry as a viable genre did not come of age artistically until the 1930s—an era, ironically, of sharp political movement toward the left and of growing political demands on literature.

One of the neglected episodes in the literary history of the early 1930s, which for political reasons has not received proper scholarly attention in China until recently, concerns a loose grouping of writers who were associated with the journal *Xiandai* (*The Contemporary* or its preferred French title, *Les contemporains,* 1932–35) and its sequel *Xinshi* (*New Poetry,* 1936–37). They wished to remain nonpartisan politically and avant-gardist artistically, waging another revolution in poetry against the early May Fourth generation. In a sense, we may consider them to be the real ancestors of poetic "modernism" in post-Mao China and, by direct descent, in Taiwan as well (one of them, Ji Xian, otherwise known as "Luyishi," went to Taiwan and began the modern poetry movement there during the 1950s).

In this regard, it may be worth quoting the words of Shi Zhi-cun, the founder and leading spokesman of *Xiandai:*

> The new poetry movement led by Mr. Hu Shi helped us to destroy the tradition of old-style Chinese poetry. However, students of new poetry from Hu Shi's time to the present have inadvertently fallen into another tradition of old-style Western poetry. They consider poetry to have rhyming patterns—at least neat poetic stanzas. Consequently, Chinese sonnets and "square-shaped" poetry are still being written by those who adhere strictly to their norms. How is this different from filling the lines of a *ci* form? The poems in *The Contemporary* are largely rhymeless, and their lines are not neatly metrical, but they all have rather fine texture. They represent the shape of modern poetry; they *are* poetry!

Shi also argued that the poetic meaning of this new free-verse form cannot and should not be easily understood at first reading. Who would have imagined that the argument would be reversed half a century later to attack the so-called obscurist poetry written by a younger generation for being "hard to understand"!

By present-day standards, this debate offers nothing striking. What makes it historically significant is its explicit challenge to a long tradition of Chinese poetry with strict regulations concerning rhyme and meter, a tradition that was not entirely broken by Hu Shi's first Literary Revolution. Also, by raising the issue of poetic texture, Shi Zhicun shifted the focus of discussion from "external" formal restrictions to the internal essence of poetry itself. For what is "texture"—a term that Shi supplied in both English and Chinese (*jili*)—if not poetic language? Moreover, in arguing that the "meaning" of modern poetry cannot be easily understood at first reading, he was also reacting against the typical reading habit of equating the poetic "content" with a "reality" outside the poem, often the reader's own commonsense perceptions. This reaction represented a first step toward separating the poetic art from ordinary "life." But Shi was too modest a poet and his meager poetic output does not lend enough weight to his arguments. The place of honor he willingly yielded to Dai Wangshu, the group's reigning poet, and to half a dozen poets who regularly contributed to *Xiandai* and later rallied around the new poetry journal *Xinshi:* Bian Zhilin, Sun Dayü, Liang Zongdai, Feng Zhi, Xu Chi, and Luyishi. This is not the place to discuss their works in detail, but a few remarks may shed light on what is to follow here.

Each in his own way, these poets attempted to evolve a poetic language—a texture, if you like—in their works. Owing to the relative plenty of Western literature that was available in Shanghai and Beijing, where most of them lived, it is not surprising that they all became eager readers of Western poetry: from Heine, Baudelaire, Mallarmé, and Rimbaud to Yeats, Pound, Eliot, Auden, and Amy Lowell. The mere list of these Western names suggests a certain indebtedness to what is generally known as Western modernism; we may even consider Dai Wangshu and his group to be the first generation of Chinese "modernists." Despite the amorphousness of the term (and its complex ramifications in a Western context), these poets did share a "modern" ethos in the sense that they saw themselves as an avant-garde, "contemporary" with the current literary trends in Europe and America. It is also not surprising that some of these Chinese modernists are now being rediscovered in post-Mao China, after half a century of neglect and ideological calumny. Dai Wangshu remains the most celebrated poet of this group.

Together with Li Jinfa, Dai is widely regarded as one of the pioneers of Chinese symbolism, a result of their early exposure to

French influences. Yet despite Dai's avowed admiration for French symbolist poets and his work translating portions of Baudelaire's *Les fleurs du mal,* his own poetry shows more traces of influence from some less well-known post-symbolists—Remy de Gourmont, Paul Fort, Francis Jammes, and Jules Superviélle—whose soft impressionistic tone poems depicting the French countryside were more palatable to his lyrical taste and whose language was perhaps also easier to comprehend. Most of Dai's own poems are lyrical in a superficial sense, offering the reader some gently mellifluent evocations of nature. His "symbolist" technique perhaps lies in investing a common object—a lighted cigarette, an old chalkbox, a half-full wine bottle—with a certain metaphorical meaning. Compared with the early works of Li Jinfa, Dai's musical-sounding lines read much more smoothly, and hence they are more accessible to the general reader—without any of the jolting, often ungrammatical phrases and bizarre images that Li piled into his exotic poems.

However, as I have mentioned earlier, before Dai Wangshu and the others reached full maturity as poets, their sociopolitical environment had changed to such an extent that they were not able to devote their full energies to the refinement of a poetic art. Nor would they have felt morally justified in doing so. In the face of an impending Japanese invasion, nonpolitical poetry writing came to be viewed as an exercise of escape in the "ivory tower," and the majority of Chinese poets—including Dai Wangshu and Bian Zhilin—chose instead to write poetry for use as a propaganda tool to arouse the masses. And the war that finally broke out in 1937 all but put an end to two decades of fertile, though uneven, poetic experimentation.

It was not until half a century later that the antecedents of modernism became relevant once more as a new generation of post-Mao poets began to move away from reality and to locate new poetic symbols against a landscape of ideological ruin.

2

The history of Chinese revolutionary and post-revolutionary art and literature under the influence of Maoism is a much better known story than the one I have sketched above, even for the Western reader. The notion of socialist realism in its Maoist guise was first canonized at the famous Talks at the Yan'an Forum on Art and Literature of 1942, where Mao stipulated in no uncertain terms that the main purpose shared by writers and artists was to praise the people, whom he defined as an aggregation of "peasants, workers, and soldiers." With an intentionally populist slant on the Soviet model, Mao not only emphasized the bright side of the revolutionary reality, which he said writers must extol, but also placed top priority on the "people" as the guiding principle for all of literature and art. Mao went on to say that writers should no longer be considered individual "artists" but rather "cultural workers," and that the sole function of literature is to serve the people. In poetry, this meant that the so-called native forms derived from folk operas and folk songs should be the models for emulation and assimilation. One such folk form, known as the "rice-sprout song" (yangge), was especially promoted by the Party. Moreover, the notion of a popular audience assumed paramount importance: poetry must not only be written for and understood by such an audience but should, so to speak, closely follow the oral mode—or better, it should be voiced aloud in front of the people. Thus instead of the refined "textures" of poetic language, poetry must reproduce a popular "tongue" and retell a formulaic story derived from a revolutionary "master narrative."

With significant political consequences, Mao's literary canon had altered entirely the modern (May Fourth and 1930s) literary "mode of production," which was based on the notions of the writer's individual talent and the value of the text. Since poetry must now contain a political message and tell a story, most poems written after the Yan'an period became literally longer and longer, like narratives. Ai Qing's famous work "Dayanhe," which glorifies the life-story of the poet's wet nurse and its rural setting, is but the most celebrated example. One can indeed be deeply moved by such a piece, especially if it is rendered orally by a committed poet-performer. The impact of this type of poetry becomes, therefore, a matter of emotional and collective identification with the subject of the poem rather than one of aesthetic distance—a privileged position from which to savor the poetic language, to derive satisfaction solely from the "pleasures of the text." In other words, the conception of modern poetry as an independent artistic enterprise became utterly alien to the Maoist mentality.

However, adherence to the Maoist canon does not fully explain the predominance of what may be called the rural mode in Chinese poetry after Yan'an. The reasons lie deeper. We must recall that in classical Chinese poetry and painting, the prevailing motif was also rural: this was especially true of the so-called landscape poetry (*shan-shui shi* or "poetry of mountains and rivers"). In the early May Fourth period Chinese intellectuals expressed special interest in folklore research, and the "voice of the people" assumed increasing significance in the literary polemics of the 1930s as a central issue for imaginative writing: how to depict the people and bring their authentic voice into literary texts by using local dialects and popular phrases? how to make the language of literature more accessible and understandable to the people? (Some writers wanted to eliminate the written Chinese script altogether and "latinize" the Chinese language.) The bulk of realistic fiction produced during the twenties and thirties was intended to reflect a rural reality. With the outbreak of the war against Japan (and long before Pearl Buck popularized it in the West), the image of the "good earth" ravaged by war and famine became a recurrent presence in most works of poetry and fiction: rural populism in literature was reinforced by a nationalistic or patriotic meaning. This is, of course, a familiar story known to all Chinese readers.

The rural mainstream of modern Chinese poetry, whether of a realistic or a revolutionary bent, is amply represented in this anthology. In a way, with some exceptions it is the primary source for all the styles of the generations of poets who came to prominence before the Cultural Revolution. However, there is also considerable diversity within this mainstream. In generational terms, some of the older poets—Ai Qing again is the best example—had been exposed to the influences of Whitman, Emile Verhaeren, Rimbaud, Mayakovsky, Esenin, and other symbolists and surrealists before they felt compelled by political circumstances, particularly the outbreak of the Sino-Japanese War, to change radically their poetic orientation from modernism to rural realism. On the other hand, some poets of the middle generation—Yan Yi, Liu Shahe, Shao Yanxiang, and Lei

Shuyan—share a less cosmopolitan background than their predecessors and tend to be influenced more by traditional Chinese conventions of meter and rhyme. In this category we should also include folk poets who either set new lyrics or narratives to traditional folk melodies or put some of the themes and materials of folk poetry into free verse poems. Still, a few poets defy grouping altogether. The translators of this anthology think so highly of Cai Qijiao's distinctive style that they are undertaking to translate a book-length selection of his poems. But the woman poet Zheng Min deserves equal attention in my judgment because, among other unusual credentials, she was among the best Western-educated writers of her generation, having received a master's degree from Brown University. Fluent in English, she is one of the few surviving members (together with Yuan Kejia, the famous poet-translator who reintroduced Western modernist literature to China shortly after Mao's death) of a group of nine highly intellectual poets who continued to write in a somewhat modernist style that was contrary to the rural revolutionary mainstream during the 1940s. Their unusual record of achievement, in quality if not in quantity, is now being reaffirmed in post-Mao China, along with the artistic contribution of slightly older poets like Dai Wangshu and Bian Zhilin.

Yet in the eyes of the truly post-Mao generation—those young poets born "under the Red Flag" (after 1949) who grew up during the chaos of the Cultural Revolution—the works of these older poets, whether native or cosmopolitan in their inspiration, all look terribly traditional (though the new poets show a grudging respect for their elders). For these younger poets, the socialist reality has been "contaminated" by an excessive ideology, so much so that ideology has served to alienate the human being from his or her true self. Thus for Bei Dao, Mang Ke, Yang Lian, Gu Cheng and other poets of this first post-Mao generation, the function of poetry is first of all to recover the human self. The following words of Gu Cheng are worth quoting because they form part of a new generation's poetic manifesto:

> I think what makes this new poetry so new is that there appears in it a "self"—a self with the special features of modern youth. . . . The new "self" is born precisely on the ruins [of the old]. He has broken

the shell that forced him to be alienated, and he flexes his body in a wind that is devoid of the fragrance of flowers. He believes in the scars of his wounds, believes in his brain and nerves, believes in walking as a master of himself.

From early samples of their poetry we can easily trace a genealogy of self-discovery: from gingerly efforts at self-portraiture ("I have these two eyes / One side is darkness / On the other side light" —Mang Ke, "Self-Portrait") to a humanistic declaration of self ("I'm not a hero / In an era without heroes / I just wanted to be a man"—Bei Dao, "Declaration"), to the defiant assertion of self as a gesture of ideological disillusionment ("Let me tell you, world / I do —not—believe!"—Bei Dao, "The Answer"). In trying to recover and redefine the self, these young poets are also fashioning a new poetic reality with their imagistic language. It may be said that these young pioneers are all beginners who, having boldly renounced the "old" revolutionary poetic tradition, are starting from scratch. Like painters in front of their new blank canvases, they first play with colors and perspectives in order to capture a transitory scene or mood (often gray, somber, and misty). As William Tay has shown, this approach is reminiscent of the strategy that was employed by the Anglo-American imagists. To reaffirm the self, they also infuse this new poetic landscape with personal emotions, especially sentiments of love (as in the works of Shu Ting). And when we view nature (sky, rain, mist, river) together with sentiment through an impressionistic prism, we are reminded of the early works of Dai Wangshu, the neglected symbolist now rediscovered. The affinity is both obvious and striking.

What gives this new type of *menglong shi* (obscurist poetry, as critics labeled it) its distinct imprint, however, is not just its scenic "mistiness" but also its further effort to compensate for the deficit. Having painted a landscape in grayish colors, the poet goes on to darken it with somber subjective associations. For this generation of poets who suffered through the Cultural Revolution, the landscape no longer looks beauteous or splendid—it has become the clear projection of a disillusioned mentality. In Yang Lian's poem-cycles ("Bell on the Frozen Lake," for instance), descriptions of famous historical sites such as the Goose Pagoda are turned into allegories of suffering and imprisonment. Poetic images do not conceal the poet's sentiments but instead serve as their direct projections. In this sense, their evocation of a collective "wasteland" is anchored in the strikingly "real" context of history and sentiment, and not (as critics have charged) in an "obscure" maze of language. But this is a very different "wasteland" from that of Eliot's famous poem.

Though not comparable to the modernist poetry of Eliot, structurally the poetry of this new generation is nevertheless different from much of Chinese traditional and folk poetry. In some ways it harks back to the free verse modes that were advocated by Shi Zhicun and practiced by the poets of the *Xiandai* group during the 1930s. Nearly all of this "modern" poetry is written in free verse without established stanzaic patterns or a regular number of characters per line. A phrase or sentence may run over from one line to the next; such enjambment is generally uncharacteristic of earlier Chinese poetry and reveals a clearly Western influence. Like their Western counterparts, the new poets also frequently omit punctuation, requiring the reader to guess where one idea ends and another begins. Besides exploiting syntactic ambiguity, the poets allow the connections between images sometimes to remain implicit. Some of the poets experiment with rhyme, but hardly with the rigorous symmetry and parallel structure that are exemplified in classical poetry. Having minimal reference to classical phraseology, these poets have preferred to create new images cast in original diction—a challenge indeed for many readers who are used to poems in the popular realistic style.

It is perhaps for this reason that the new poetry was interpreted as "obscure" and hard to comprehend by no less an established writer than Ai Qing. Still, the ambiguity that he and his colleagues censured is also abundant in classical poetry, and even in some of their own earlier works. Perhaps the real cause of their attack was that they felt threatened by an apparent indifference toward the political commitment that had dominated socialist poetry for over thirty years. Once alerted, Party cadres also worried that obscurity might possibly be a screen for criticism of the current regime.

Among writers even younger than the obscurists, various traditional and modern philosophical underpinnings are manifest. For instance, Wang Xiaolong in Shanghai and Tang Yaping in Sichuan have developed a distinctive approach that could be called "non-emotionalization" *(wu qing hua)*. Their poems echo the existentialist viewpoint that man possesses no special privilege, much less divine sanction, in the universe; human beings have no more significance than an insect does. Or as Lao Zi believed, the universe is not humane and treats everything as it treats a dog. Removing man from center stage as the measure of all things, Wang and Tang make a departure from the humanism that is implicit in much of the work by other poets in this anthology, including the obscurists, and in this respect their work more closely approximates Western modernism. Writing more colloquially than Bei Dao, Wang Xiaolong portrays love as an important feeling, but one no less common or vulgar than other feelings. His poem "When We Finally Turn Fifty" catalogues the ordeals of daily conjugal life and suggests a comparison between lovers sleeping "with our heads stuck together" and their dream of "two small dogs running across the snow." Tang Yaping masterfully delves into black humor, another trait of the so-called non-emotive writers.

But a humanistic kind of detachment occurs in the more popular approach of Yu Jian, whose poems focus on life in the mountains and hinterlands. An American counterpart for his writing might be found in some of Ernest Hemingway's stories about men struggling for survival—in particular *The Old Man and the Sea,* which is widely read in China. Yu Jian's understatement of emotion produces strong undercurrents of feeling hidden behind a screen of offhand detachment. The future development of all these young writers deserves critical attention.

From their stance opposite the obscurists, this younger generation of poets—who are only in their twenties and too young to have experienced the full impact of the Cultural Revolution—are criticizing their predecessors for, among other things, being too historically conscious and too ornate in their poetic imagery. Some of the young challengers would like to go a step further and strip poetry of all social or cultural references so that it can be truly free and "pure." One of the leading groups of such younger poets, from the western province of Sichuan, named their new poetry journal *Fei Fei*—literally "No No" and figuratively a close equivalent to dadaism! Another group of poets, who live in Shanghai, are experimenting with what they call "urban consciousness" by attempting to develop a certain rhythm and imagery that will approximate the dynamism and chaotic sensations of city living. Still others, such as the poet and folk singer Cui Jian, are reaching a much larger and less intellectual audience with simple but cleverly daring and satirical lyrics that mock the solemnity of all official symbols. (Cui Jian set his song "Nothing to My Name" to a rock beat but performed it in public dressed in army and peasant garb recalling the Yan'an era!) And a young Mongolian poet whom I met in 1986 gave me a mimeographed copy of his recent work, a simple prose poem that described a personal experience of epiphany in a public latrine at night when the electricity suddenly went out.

Extreme individualism coupled with an anarchic impulse informs the works of this youngest generation—something that would have been very difficult to imagine even during the early years of the post-Mao period. Although this anthology cannot include as many poems by them as by earlier poets, the samples appearing here may still be sufficient to give readers an inkling of what is to come in the Chinese poetry scene—a diversity of extreme sensibilities, a polyphony of new voices clamoring to be heard, a raw energy and a defiant spirit that can no longer be contained by any official campaigns. Given more time, China's younger poets will surely bring out a rich and varied harvest of poetic creation, the likes of which has not been witnessed during the past forty years. If we combine this new poetic outpouring from the mainland with the equally fertile productivity of poetry written in Taiwan since the early 1950s (available in English translation in several anthologies), we may be prepared to predict that the day will come when the "modern" corpus of new poetry produced amid the chaos of the twentieth century can indeed challenge the long and splendid tradition of classical Chinese poetry.

LEO OU-FAN LEE
Center for Far Eastern Studies
The University of Chicago
March 1989

POSTSCRIPT

Since the Beijing massacre and crackdown, begun on June 3, 1989, by Deng Xiaoping and Li Peng, the practice of literature has changed drastically in the People's Republic of China. Freedom of publication has virtually ceased, and many writers—like other intellectuals—have exited the country or indefinitely postponed their return from foreign studies and travel. This pattern is most evident among the younger writers: three of the four major "obscurist poets" currently are living abroad, and several less well-established young poets have also shown up in cities outside China.

Such calamities have occurred before, and Chinese literature has nevertheless survived. The brief freedom of the Hundred Flowers period (1956 through early 1957) was followed by anti-rightist persecutions in 1957 and the ensuing deep freeze of the Cultural Revolution (1966–76). The Beijing Spring of 1978–79 eventually prompted the regime's largely unsuccessful "Campaign against Spiritual Pollution" in 1982. While the government now campaigns to reeducate the intellectuals, some expatriate writers are practicing politics as vigorously as they once produced literature.

The personal and literary disruption caused by the recent upheaval cannot be fully estimated at this time. Will writers who flourished in China during the last dozen years become permanent expatriates? Will they become assimilated into other cultures to such an extent that they develop incompletely as artists of their native idiom? Perhaps the next generation of writers on the mainland already has lost its best teachers of literature.

The past twelve years since the end of the Cultural Revolution may emerge as a distinct, pivotal time in Chinese cultural history because the window of freedom opened wider and for a longer period than at any time since before the Sino-Japanese War. It is not inconceivable that valuable works written during these few years may be turning up as classics for some time to come. Although the government's repression has removed the minimal safeguards to artistic freedom most writers need for imaginative work, the devices of thought control that were prevalent during the Maoist period seem out of the question for the time being. The country's leadership has lost credibility, if not legitimacy, in the minds of too many citizens for that kind of control to succeed.

Just as the Chinese literature of the past has weathered storms of adversity and calamity, modern Chinese literature too is likely to prevail eventually on the mainland. "They can't kill us all," the recent demonstrators were saying. Let us hope that the next generation of Chinese writers is not forced to take up the cry again. What strangely innovative works will they produce living in a nation that deliberately, though sporadically, makes life within its borders intolerable for free-spirited writers?

EDWARD MORIN
September 1989

The
Red
Azalea

Ai Qing

is the pen name of Jiang Haicheng (1910–), the son of a landowner, who studied medicine and against his parents' wishes went to Paris in 1929, where he made his living by painting porcelains. His ambition turned from painting to poetry as he read the French symbolists and other modern Western poets, including Whitman and Mayakovsky. Returning to China in 1932, he became active in progressive Chinese literary circles. He was arrested in July of the same year by police of the French Concession in Shanghai for harboring "dangerous ideas" and wrote many well-known poems in prison.

In 1941 he went to Yan'an, capital of the area then held by the Chinese Communist Party, and soon espoused Mao Zedong's principle that literature must serve the revolution by portraying the people and their revolutionary leaders favorably. He was chief editor of *Poetry Magazine* and became China's best-known poet. During the 1950s he was associate editor of *People's Literature*. In 1957 the Party charged him with being a rightist and for twenty years kept him isolated, mainly in Xinjiang. Although he was not prevented from writing poetry, all the poems he wrote during that period have been lost.

Ai Qing returned to Beijing in 1975 and began to publish poems again in 1978 after the fall of the "Gang of Four." In 1979 he became vice-chairman of the Chinese Writers' Association. When Bei Dao and other young poets began publishing their new poetry in the late 1970s, Ai Qing joined the well-known elderly poets Zang Kejia and Yuan Shuipai in publicly denouncing the alleged obscurantism and anti-socialist stance of the "obscurist poets." His own reputation, however, has suffered since the obscurists have gained an enthusiastic audience, especially on university campuses.

Ai Qing has published at least fourteen books of poetry. His major works are *The Selected Poems of Ai Qing* (Beijing, 1952) and a collection of essays entitled *On Poetry* (Beijing, 1955). A selection of his poetry, translated into English by Eugene Chen Eoyang, has been published as *Selected Poetry of Ai Qing* (Indiana University Press, 1982).

The City

The city has its own scenery of peaks and wildernesses

A landscape of gentle hills
And large low blocks of one-story houses
The sheer cliffs and overhanging rocks in the distance
Are range after range of concrete mountains

When was Yunnan's rocky moraine
Moved down here
Those multi-storied buildings
How unassailable are they

The city's countless streets and lanes
Are so many rivers and brooks
People mill about all day long
Like river water surging and roiling

Throughout the city
Like the splashing of waterfalls
Like the onrush of a train
Like the circling of a plane in the sky
Thousands of sounds reverberate

As the curtain of night settles, the windows
Suddenly beam their glittering lights
And the city becomes the largest of stages
On which every imaginable person performs

Selected Poetry of 1981

Swan Lake

A feathery shudder
The supple grace of movements hard to capture
Leaps of pure whiteness
Like light rays caroming through a woods

Love pursuing
Shyness escaping
Rapture trembling
The pull of deep feeling

Lake water tender as dusk
Misty as the grove of trees encircling the lake
As if starlight glimmering in the night sky
Were flitting from place to place in musical notes

MAY 5, 1980

Selected Poetry of 1981

Dreams

Waking hours
Are crammed with fantasy
Then dreams
Drop in to visit while you sleep

Perhaps an early childhood sweetheart
Or an old buddy arriving from far away

Grief writhes on an inner-spring mattress
Ecstatic rendezvous occur on a heap of straw

While poverty-stricken you receive gifts
When you're affluent you get robbed

It could be a false alarm
Or the inkling that more is amiss

SPRING 1980

People's Literature (Renmin Wenxue), no. 3 (March 1981)

Bonsai

As if left over from ancient times
These plants have been mineralized
Trunks of bronze, branches of iron wire
Even their leaves are colored verdigris
In an old-fashioned squared-off courtyard
They don't suffer from cold in winter or heat in summer
Their stands of sandalwood and padauk
Project them into stances for special notice

It's clear they are hapless artifacts
That long ago lost their natural color
Suffering under subjection and high-handed treatment
In all sorts of planting pots
Every step in their growing process
Has been fraught with wire-and-scissors torture
Not free to expand, they let others push them around
Part of them developed, part withered
Standardized into disequilibrium

Handicapped specimens
Like many rachitic old people
Whom others point out for their grotesque shapes
Some with distended bellies
Others with exposed roots
Bearing a few finely curved twigs
Sesame-sized leaves barely suggest a trace of youth
And several prop up their disabled lives
Like wounded soldiers who've endured their limit of battle fire

Yet all flowers and trees
Ought to have their own ground
Roots need to absorb nutrients from the soil
Leaves and branches want rain, dew and sunshine

They should develop freely and naturally
Have peace of mind in the open air
Accepting nature's caresses
Sending out their own fragrances

But everything gets turned upside down
The young become old, the old act young
To satisfy people's curiosity
And to flaunt the techniques of proprietary gardeners
Twisted because they're easily twirled around fingers
And cut viciously by knives because plants have no tongues
Maybe this mistreatment is also a kind of art
But its productions are a broken-down travesty of freedom

FEBRUARY 23, 1979

Songs of the Return (Guilai de Ge)

Hope

A friend of dreams
And sister of fantasy

She is your very shadow
But always walks ahead

Shapeless as pure light
Restless as the wind

There is always some distance
Between the two of you

Like a bird flying outside the window
Or a cloud sailing in air

Like the butterfly beside the river
Cagey yet exquisite

Go after her—she'll fly away
Ignore her—she'll chase you

She'll always keep you company
Until your breathing stops

Ai Qing

Umbrella

One morning I asked the umbrella
Whether it would rather bake in the sun
Or stand soaking in the rain.

The umbrella answered with a smile,
"Those things don't bother me."

I kept on questioning,
"Then what is your concern?"

The umbrella said,
"I keep thinking
On rainy days, 'Don't let people's clothes get wet,'
And on sunny days, 'Be a cloud that shades their heads.' "

Ai Qing

Figure Skating

Flower of winter
Carnival for the cold

On an off-white surface
Appears a figure of perfect beauty

This lightness of poise
Produces the most elegant dancing

Along floating points
You've painted a floating line

Gently sweeping arcs
Swift and subtle turns

Sudden jumps while spinning
Sudden spins while jumping

Restless flying
Graceful whirling

Calm as a soaring eagle
Nimble as a diving swallow

A fantasy of dynamics
Geometric obsession

Music with no rests
Poem with no stops

Expansive as flowing water
Continuous as turning wheels

AI QING   II

Leaping into air
Limbs become flower petals

Freer than the wind
Celebrating youth

Ai Qing

Liquor

She is lovely
With a personality of fire
And a shape like water

This nymph of happiness
Deigns to visit
Where people are celebrating

She's an expert tease
Able to make you tell the truth
And pluck out what's deepest in your heart

She can make you
Forget your afflictions
And be completely happy

For victory, drink
For friendship, drink
For love, drink

Still you have to be careful
Or she'll pilfer your mind
During your merriest hours

Don't gaze upon her as water
To extinguish your grief
For she's oil poured onto fire

She can make bright people clever
And fools ever more foolish

Ai Qing

Echo

She's hiding in the valley
She's standing over the cliff
If you refuse to dally
She'll act as if she's deaf

But call her and she'll call you
Curse her and you she'll curse
You can't win if you argue
The last word's always hers

Ai Qing

Cai Qijiao

(1918–) was born in Fujian Province and in 1926 emigrated with his parents to Indonesia, returning to China by himself at age eleven to attend school in Fujian. After high school, he went home to Indonesia, returned to China again in 1938, and later walked with friends all the way from Wuhan to Yan'an. He worked among soldiers in the New Fourth Army, then entered Lu Xun Arts Academy where he studied literature. He began to teach in 1940 and to write poetry in 1941. When the novelist Ding Ling founded the Central Literature Training Institute in 1952, Cai headed its teaching and research office of foreign literature.

His seven collections of poetry include three that were published during the Hundred Flowers and Anti-Rightist era of 1957–58: *Echoes, The Sound of Waves,* and *A Further Collection of Echoes.* He was criticized for writing mainly about scenery, people, and love, with too little regard for the political line of the Party.

During the Cultural Revolution, he was again condemned for refusing to write conventional Marxist poems praising the heroes of class struggle and denouncing landlords. Critics found the romantic associations of his water imagery deficient because they expected him to rhapsodize about dams and hydroelectric plants. He is rare among poets who lived in the People's Republic during the Cultural Revolution because he persisted in writing personal poetry, although scarcely any of it was published or even shown until afterwards. His prolific output since the Cultural Revolution includes the poetry collections *Prayer* (1981), *Songs of Life* (1982), *Facing the Wind* (1984), and *The Drunken Stone* (1986). He has worked at the Fujian Federation of Literary and Arts Circles and has travelled extensively throughout China. His home is in Beijing, and he winters in Fujian.

The Pearl

is the oyster's wound—
A rough, hard obstruction
Intrudes into its tender body.
Month by month, year after year,
Wrapped in layer upon adhesive layer,
It becomes round, glistening, smooth, glossy.
Crystalized pain, a tear shed by the sea,
Yet all the mundane treasure it!
I sense that it still wears the salt smell of the ocean,
That this glistening teardrop bears
The grief of sun and moon, stars and clouds.

1979

The People's Daily (Ren Min Ri Bao), June 12, 1979

Distance

Lying between the real and the imagined
You are a mountain flaming with red leaves,
Sadness and joy confounded at dusk;
You are forest shadow, evening breeze
And darkness on the way home.

Lying between the real and the imagined
You are the wild goose keeping its promise,
An unexpected meeting in the street;
You are delightful laughter, brilliant light,
A night capped with a show of fireworks.

Lying between the real and the imagined
You are translucent white sculpture,
Deep sleep illumined by good fortune;
You are a subtle fragrance, you are flowers,
The generosity of selfless Nature.

Lying between the real and the imagined
You are a complaint without a reason,
Painful longing on a gloomy rainy day;
You are a cool moon, remote star,
The abyss too mysterious to fathom.

Poetry Magazine (Shikan), no. 7 (July 1981)

Longing

My longing for you brims with feelings of spring—
A clear flowing stream
Ripples in the foreground,
The green landscape beyond
Stretches back into the distance,
Under the quiet shadow of a cloud
Your smile is like the passage of fluttering birds.

My longing for you never rests—
As the rising moon
Skims over layer after layer of branches
You walk out from the depths of my heart
And through layer upon layer of memories
You cast radiant light on everything around me.

My longing for you comes back to reality—
On the mountain a high tower
Quiet under a hazy drizzle,
Waiting thus forever for love,
Without so much as a word
Without even hinting my intentions.

Long Spring (Chang Chun), no. 8 (August 1979)

Poetry

It is the tide, an everlasting cry,
Or a star, the never-ending silence.
Whether shouted or voiceless,
Neither is for human beings to choose.

How easy to not write poetry for truth.
Lies come along to cover emptiness.
The shining flower petals of glory
Are not the same thing as the truth.

To search the heart is poetry's lifeblood.
Perhaps it was found but it's been lost again.
The blue smoke and grey ash—
Both are brothers of that fire.

MARCH 7, 1976

Praying

Painted Landscape

Between deep snow and melting ice a brook
Treads a line voicing joyous songs of life

The green-clothed wilderness guards a straight highway
Groaning of the bond between light and shadow

The wistful setting sun shrouded in haze
Murmurs among lush boughs of the tall trees

In still mountain woods waterfalls cascade
Scattering hollow echoes in the distance

Whether summer rain slants or winter snow flies
Each of them sends forth vibrant melodies

Even the naked trees in silent darkness
Seem to moan somehow in their secrecy

To extract from ten thousand hues only the innocent
Crystalizes nature's color and sound

To recreate foam in the deep valley's torrent
Requires a most profound love of life.

1978

Anhui Literature (Anhui Wenxue), no. 2 (February 1979)

I Want

Don't you believe the silence in the stone,
It's not so tranquil when the wind blows by,
But hopelessly looks up at rose-hued clouds
And sighs with all its might for that vast distance.
If space will allow
Clouds to produce rain
Let the stone erode into deep grottos
And weather into gritty detritus!

Don't you believe the autumn leaf's indifference,
Even though it's withered well past yellow;
When the moment for departure arrives
It will also be sobbing to green leaves.
If time will allow
Fallen leaves to gather,
Lay your tired head upon them!
Hide your shaking hand in them!

1979

Songs of Life

The Wasteland

Monotonous, quiet.
A swath of scrubland, rows of hills and bluffs,
Scattered saplings gently question the sky:
In other places people's roads connect—
Why don't they care enough to do that here?
Only rain to moisten this sandy earth,
Clouds dark as mountains look about sadly.

MARCH 2, 1979

Songs of Life

Still Praying

I pray for a breeze in sweltering summer,
A little less precipitation in winter.
May the flowers bloom red, purple, or whatever;
May love be spared derisive laughter,
May someone be available to prop up the fallen.
Let me have compassionate people around
So that when a man is really down
They at least won't increase his pain
By turning a cold shoulder and arched eyebrows;
Each day of the year, like a cooling spring
Gushing forth non-stop, let us have some wisdom,
Instead of bans and rulings against this or that.
I ask to hear songs welling from the heart
Without someone laying down a formula
Of prearranged keys for every melody.
I pray
For the day when people will have no need
To pray the way I have had to do here.

APRIL 16, 1975

Creative Works (Zuoping), no. 1 (January 1979)

The Desert Wind

Blasting across the boundless Gobi Desert
Accompanied by a deep virile melody
Strong wind ruffling countless strands of my thought
Would you be softer and a bit more gentle!

Everything that grows to ripeness must sweat blood
In this territory of hunger and thirst
Must windblown sand always cover the road
From blossom time until the fruit has ripened?

The hard years of pioneer settlement
Have drained too many people's hearts of blood
The yelling gale that soars into the sky
Is not just part of some eternal game

Fervor without reason vaults to the blue-gray sky
Indifferent in its thrusts at good or evil
It breaks huge boulders into pebbles
With one roar rolling everything down flat

The clank of swords and sabers
Shakes earth and sky and sweeps toward emptiness
Blackened shadows steadily advance
But no trace is left of our glorious past

The clouds of war are plunged across the world
While spume and muddy waves pitch and roar
Hold your breath and listen
Do these things show the destiny of generations?

The wind is changing now from south to north
Sparse raindrops riddle the desert sand
Huge clouds roll by like waves on the high seas
Moist shadows of lightning flash across the Gobi

Shaking the dark locks of your hair
Thundering your challenges into the air
Persistent wind churning among the clouds
Would you please be softer, a bit more gentle!

September 12, 1985

Poetry Magazine (Shikan), no. 4 (April 1986)

Memory

An ice-cold river encircles the log hut
Whose compassionate face is staring toward me.
A tree like an umbrella shields the river
Who with windlike fingers plucks my heartstrings.

You are a bright cloud in my evening sky
While I sing you a poem about sunset.
But your songs are constellations of stars
That go on flickering deep in my soul.

My poem is merely withering leaves
Who in a warm dream laugh at thunderstorms,
But your songs are like the silence of flowers
Whose lasting fragrance scorns authority.

The Double Rainbow

Zheng Min

(1920–) was born in Beijing and attended the National Southwest Associated University in Kunming during World War II. A philosophy major, she also was known for her fine singing voice. Her elegant and polished writing style owes something to the example of Feng Zhi and Bian Zhilin, who were also at the university when she was a student. She published about sixty poems, written between 1942 and 1947, in a volume entitled *The Poems (Shi Ji)* (Shanghai, 1949).

Continuing her education in the United States, she received a master's degree in English literature from Brown University in 1951. In 1959 she and her husband, an engineer, returned home to China, where they suffered harassment from government authorities who suspected them of being American spies. For many years Zheng Min taught English language, but not literature, and she also stopped writing poetry during the Cultural Revolution.

She has since resumed writing poetry and, until her recent retirement, taught literature as a professor of English at Beijing Normal University. She is a member of the Chinese Writers' Association. Her work has appeared in the Chinese periodicals *Poetry* and *Stars* and in *Water in Autumn* in the United States. She has edited several anthologies of poetry and has published a volume of critical studies on English and American poetry and drama. Translations of her poems have appeared in *The Penguin Book of Women's Poetry* and other anthologies.

Repairing the Wall

> Before I built a wall I'd ask to know
> What I was walling in or walling out.
>
> —Robert Frost, *Mending Wall*

Half a century has passed. In spring
People are restoring and repairing the fence,
But there is no contention.
Neighbors all agree to repair a wall or mend a fence.
What is to be walled in
And what is to be walled out?

No arguments here.
The civilization our ancestors left us
Must be encircled and all barbarism and wildness excluded:
Quiet countryside,
Energetic morning,
Fluttering birds in the distance,
Soundless bells in Big Bell Temple,
The Fragrant Hills spreading wellwater
Over people's souls; the understanding smile
Of the arhat, poetry of pine trees
Are words that don't have to be said.

The painter's brush alive in people's hearts,
The ancient Chinese lute played in people's souls,
Civilization glowing in the roots of our nation—
For all these, people are repairing a wall
Or mending a fence in springtime.

So what—if foxes clench their teeth outside the wall,
No matter that wolves howl outside the wall,
For we have repaired our own great wall.

Yangtze River (Chang Jiang), no. 1 (January 1981)

Pearls

How many years have you slept on the sea bottom!
Time has not passed in vain,
A rainbow of light flashing over your uneven shell
Glitters freely, suffused in coral pink.
A true pearl
Is not the most perfect one.

Pearls cultivated on a production schedule
Have a regular, plump-eared surface.
A handful of them, all the same size,
Show off their brilliance encircling
Pretty wrists and necks; they are most perfect,
But they are not real pearls.

Nothing seems more like pearls than virtue does:
The truest probably don't look the most beautiful,
The most beautiful probably aren't the truest.
My heart and soul are always
Enchanted by the uneven pearl
Because it carries messages from the ocean
And owns a sincerity for which I yearn.

1982

Yangtze River (Chang Jiang), no. 1 (January 1981)

A Mother's Heart in Autumn

The autumn sun hesitates in longing,
Willow switches slowly relax their grip,
Allowing summer's greenery to quietly fall.
The brook is exceptionally clear and calm
So that it may reflect the deeper thoughts
Of awakened philosophers and of all the world.
I carefully pressed a rooted sprig of rose
Into soil that was becoming colder with each day.

I saw a young man standing at the gate of hope
Saying goodbye to his mother,
Whose glances locked into mine.
Although north winds soon will howl like wild wolves
And white snow may float onto that son's grave,
I still carefully pack the rose cutting
Into soil that is colder day by day.
Let the lives of the young be severely tested—
Only bitter memories of winter roots
Can make us long for spring blossoming.

AUTUMN 1981

Yangtze River (Chang Jiang), no. 1 (January 1981)

Yan Yi

(1927-) is from the far western province of Sichuan. He joined the Eighth Route Army led by the Chinese Communist Party in 1942 and published his first book of poems in 1949. In all, he has published over thirty books of his poetry, plays, screenplays, criticism, and other prose. A volume of his selected poems has appeared, entitled *The Snow Welcomes Immigrating Wild Geese*. He is editor of *Selected Lyrics of Contemporary China* and co-editor of *Selected Modern Short Poetry*—two anthologies in Chinese, both published in 1984. He works for a film studio in Sichuan.

In an Airplane

Ascending, I left noisy earth behind,
Ascending, I passed through sea clouds and mountain clouds.
Ascending, I met the tranquil blue sky,
Ascending, I entered the freedom of high altitude.
But altitude is merely empty space.
My heart falls back to the busy, disordered human world.
The upper air is clear, uncontaminated,
Yet indifferent as ice, without human warmth.
There is endless isolation and quiet,
Yet no irksome jealousy or deception.
Although thinking isn't prohibited,
There is no heart-to-heart talk with friends,
No path strewn with flowers for me to walk,
No fertile fields to work with plow or sickle.
A seat belt shackles me into my armchair,
This cagelike freedom is stifling my feelings.
Let me go back to earth,
Where grief—such as it is—claims half of life;
The other half is cheerful laughter, fiery hope
Surpassing what's in the sky, more beautiful than dreams.

SEPTEMBER 4, 1979

The Southern Tree

32   YAN YI

Sketches of a Metropolis

I

How many tires ten million people own!
On the avenue they are all looking for
Speed—the top priority of our time.

II

Yet high above every intersection,
Red and green lights speak the comradely language
Of weighty love.

III

What a contradictory scene!
Some crave high speed,
Others strive to prevent it.

IV

Neither side wins total victory
Or suffers total defeat,
So the world keeps moving.

V

I dare not sing an ode to green
For fear that speed would take advantage
Of my love and run recklessly out of control.

VI

Nor dare I sing an ode to red:
It may seem more secure
But security is probably mankind's cancer.

VII

Intricate and simple learning
Both whiten the hair and eyebrows
Of many a statesman and scientist.

VIII

Maybe life on this planet is in neutral,
Speed criticizes slowness,
And slowness keeps criticizing speed.

The Snow Welcomes Immigrating Wild Geese: Selected Poetry (Xue Ying Zhenghong)

The Trolley Car Goes On

Who would have thought I'm really old enough
For young people to show me sympathy?
No sooner did I climb aboard the trolley
Than a young man stood and helped me to his seat.
I gratefully accepted and sat down,
Yet now and then my heart felt some disturbance.
It's I who should have offered him a seat—
My shoulders won't bear heavy loads again.
It's I who should have offered him a seat—
He'll carry loads far heavier than I did.
Longer, more rugged paths are waiting for him,
He'll have to scale much higher, steeper mountains!
He's the one who should have saved his strength,
But there he stood, hand locked upon the strap.
I gave the seat back to the brave young man
And shamefully got off before my stop,
Propelling myself into deepest thought,
Confounding my disturbed heart all the more.

SEPTEMBER 30, 1982

Stars (Xing Xing), no. 4 (April 1982)

Poetry Itself Is a Kind of Sunlight

Believe me, poetry itself is a kind of sunlight
No substance has been found anywhere in the cosmos
That can break the wings of poetry.
Here's a chance at last to meet one another,
The river in Shenzhen chuckles merrily
The sky sheds joyous tears.
Though we've never met before,
We can love each other with brotherly sincerity,
As if we'd lived in the same family
Ten thousand years ago.
Then, believe me, after a hundred thousand years,
We'll still be inseparable.
Yes, there is continual interweaving of poetry's sunlight
While poetry's sun and our hearts
Burn together
Warming and illuminating the cold world.

Poetry Magazine (Shikan), no. 1 (January 1987)

Liu Shahe

is the pen name of Yu Xuntan (1931–), who was born into a family of small landowners in Chengdu, capital of Sichuan Province. In 1935 the family moved back to the parents' hometown of Jintang. During the land reform campaign, the Communists killed his father because he had worked for the Nationalist government. In 1948 Liu Shahe started writing and in 1949 he became a student of agricultural chemistry at Sichuan University. The following year he was an editor of the supplement to the *Western Sichuan Peasant Daily* and he later edited *Sichuan Masses*. In 1952 he joined the Chinese New Democratic Youth League (later renamed the Communist Youth League) and started working as a professional writer. Encouraged by critics after his first poem was published in 1955, Liu Shahe started to write poetry almost exclusively. His first book of poems, *The Country Nocturnes,* was published in 1956, and he was admitted to the Academy of Literature. During that year he was also one of four editors who started publishing the monthly poetry magazine *Stars.* Two weeks after its founding, he was criticized for a series of his poems entitled "Grass and Stars" that had appeared in the magazine's first issue. These poems eventually led to his being disgraced as a rightist in 1957.

He spent the next eight years as a worker of all sorts, ranging from laborer to librarian. From 1966 to 1978 he was exiled in Jintang, where he lived without any job or income. He continued writing poems, although very few of them are preserved, and he resumed publishing in 1978. The poems of his selected for this anthology were first published after that date. His fourteen books include *Windows* (1956), a collection of stories, and *Farewell to Mars* (1957), a second collection of poems. His book *Poems of Liu Shahe* (1982) won a National Prize for Poetry. Two more of his poetry collections, *Track of the Wanderer* and *Goodbye, Hometown,* were published in 1983. Since then he has published seven books of criticism and other nonfiction.

The Eyes

Naive eyes see friends everywhere
Sullen eyes see enemies everywhere
Terrified eyes see traps everywhere
Greedy eyes see gold everywhere
Sorrowful eyes see desolation everywhere
Smiling eyes see brightness everywhere

Two eyes often struggle against each other
One is too naive
The other too sullen
Therefore the eyes behold total confusion
Enemies look like friends
And friends look like enemies

EARLY SPRING, 1957

Collected Poems

More about Eyes

People say eyes are the windows of the soul
Can you really believe that

Why is it that I'm so familiar with your eyes
But have never understood your soul

Perhaps your eyes consistently feign sincerity
Perhaps your soul can't reveal itself in public

It also may be that these two *perhaps*es are off the mark
And only I am to blame because I have never had eyes

EARLY SPRING, 1957

Collected Poems

Inscription Seen on a Trip to Bao Ji

Being misunderstood by someone
Is vexation
Being misunderstood by everyone
Is tragedy

JUNE 20, 1957

Collected Poems

A Philosophy of Saws

True. The saws are sawing wood,
But wood is also sawing the saws.
Thus saws are becoming dull—
The more they are sharpened the frailer they get,
And eventually they break.

The wood sawn into boards
Is fashioned into furniture.
Saws just break
And are discarded.

1972

Collected Poems

Shao Yanxiang

(1933-) was born in Beijing and at age sixteen left school to work at the Radio Beijing broadcasting station, just as the Chinese Communists assumed power in 1949. Less than a year later he published his first collection of poems, *Songs of Beijing City*. He wrote many poems in praise of the new China, and then in 1956 his style began to change. He wrote not only poetry, but also satirical essays *(zawen)* to expose important issues and ridicule the shortcomings of real-life officials and bureaucrats.

Because he praised and supported Wang Meng's controversial story "A Young Man Arrives at the Organization Department," he was severely criticized and denounced as a rightist during the Anti-Rightist campaign of 1957-58. He has published about nine collections of poetry, including *In a Remote Place* (1984). He is a former editor of *Poetry Magazine,* the most important poetry journal in China. He has been a writer in residence at the University of Iowa, and in the spring of 1989 visited California. He has recently been vice-chairman of the Chinese Writers' Association.

My Optimism

I'm an adult
My optimism is adult too

My optimism
Doesn't smile all the time
It has rolled in the mud
It's been struck on an anvil
It burst out into sparks under the hammer
It burned in a bonfire that almost went out
For a while people scornfully called it dead ash

It has been worked over with nightsticks
Jerked around every which way,
Then floated downriver chilled to the bone
None of its fibres
Is tainted by even a speck of dust
It doesn't wear coveralls
Not my optimism

My optimism
Isn't a coat
That you sometimes put on and then take off
Nor does it have a pocket with a conscience inside
That you could sometimes bring with you
Or sometimes leave at home

My optimism
Leaped into my arms
And I warmed it up with my body heat
After it had been trampled when those
Who had once embraced it cast it aside

I warmed it up
And it warmed me

Double-crossed
And reported on in secret
It grew up step by step
Yet without encountering obstacles
Without a taste of mean tricks
How could my optimism become adult?

Adult optimism
Isn't always sweet
Sometimes its face is bathed in tears
I once heard it choking back sobs
But it woke out of its grief
Caught my hand
Comforted my heart
Propped my head in both hands
And tried gently to console me
With a tune that only parents would use for a child
Hello old friend inseparable as body and shadow
My long-suffering weather-beaten optimism

JANUARY 28, 1984

Shanghai Literature (Shanghai Wenxue), no. 5 (May 1984)

I'll Always Remember

Thirty-three tribunals of public censure
Thirty-three bold-character posters
Thirty-three waves and thirty-three storms
Thirty-three tramplings underfoot . . .
Simply because you
Cast me a secretive glance
That would wipe away
Grief from the sky and sorrow from my heart

Sixty-six shout-downs and harassments
Sixty-six floggings and beatings
Sixty-six dismemberments and humiliations
Sixty-six torture sessions and strangulations . . .
I heard voiceless language
From your closed lips
Telling me in the dead of winter
That flowers somewhere hadn't all withered

Ninety-nine cursings
Ninety-nine wounds
Ninety-nine death sentences
Ninety-nine levels of hell . . .
Could not have overcome
Your hand stretched forth to prop me—
That wisp of tenderness
Rescued me a hundred times a hundred times

I'll always remember your bitter smile
You'll always remember my pained loyalty
Belief
Ah, my belief
Let's cast a contemptuous look
On those whose stratagems all came to naught

MARCH 18, 1981

Shanghai Literature Review (Shanghai Wenxue Bao), 1981 or 1982

River in My Dream

I have a river
My river
That flows continuously through my dreams
And changes color every so often

It flashes orange one moment and bright blue the next
Sometimes it's overflowing, sometimes clear and shallow
Here and there it splashes in white rapids

This river in my dream
Carrying my time
My happiness and sorrow
Carrying my ceaseless thoughts
And my obstinate quest

Flows during blue nights
And white snowy days
Looks for the ferryboat at a big willow
Glazed with ice residue in early spring

I've heard faraway drumming
Blows against the sides and bottom of the boat
If I were the boat
I'd cast off and hasten into midstream

Goodbye, green grass on the bank
Goodbye, white-headed reeds along the shore
Goodbye to those days when I waited impatiently to cross
And to my spring and autumn when the long current dwindled

Just when life seemed to dry up
I dreamed the spring tide flowing level with the riverbank
I dreamed the soft sounds of oars sculling
I dreamed a river rushing right past my door
And flowing into the mighty ocean
I dreamed I sat in the boat on the spring flood
As if sitting in the highest heaven
I even felt myself drifting with the current

I dreamed I stowed my plain luggage
My love and my ideals
In the bow of the boat
And I reached over the gunwale to scoop
The cold clear river water
Which belongs to me only while I dream

And I let its freshets course over my worn face
And moisten my parched singing voice

Only the continuous beat
Of the murmuring current
Makes me dream
And then wakes me up:
Freedom!
Ah
Freedom!

MAY 3, 1982

Lake Qinghai (Qinghai Hu), 1982

Untitled

That sun, that same busy sun goes on
Shining over earth twenty-four hours a day—
Don't let birds aimlessly peck this green apple
Now slowly turning red, early in autumn;
In early autumn sunshine I find this great land
Sauntering toward ripeness,
And I discover myself, and many friends too . . .
Half-ripened apples hanging on the boughs,
What is it that's ripening in my heart?

That song, that same singing voice goes on,
Melody flashing like a bolt of glittering silk—
Swirling around a regal harp, fingers pliant and tough,
Pianos, electric guitar, brocaded zither and *konghou;**
The song flows on like sunrays and moonbeams
Flowing through my heart—your bright eyes
That once lit happiness in my sad days,
Let them melt the sadness in your happy moments.

That heart, that same pair of hands goes on,
The heart joins other hearts, hand reaches for hands—
My heart is obsessed, obsessed with life,
My hand waves, waves toward friends;
Life, Friends, please don't let me down again!
I still have favors to repay, haven't yet loved enough!
In the sky, let's fly while we sing! Yes, sing!
On earth, let's run completely free! Yes, free!

OCTOBER 13, 1980

In the Remote (Zai Yuanfang)

*An ancient wind instrument

Waiting

It's no longer a fresh clear April morning
Nor is this the tract of neatly planted maples
No more sunbeams and raindrops
Are sliding simultaneously from tender
Five-tined leaves down into my collar

It's already a November evening
And even in my heart
The dreary chilling rain of autumn falls
Autumn rain pierces the broken umbrella
Of French parasol trees* scattered here and there
It patters down upon my broken umbrella
More hurriedly than the steps of passersby

Hurrying pedestrians become more and more scarce
I stand in the shadow of a misty streetlamp
Under parasol trees whose last leaves soon will fall
I stand in late autumn's night rain blown slanted by wind
And I wait for you

It's no longer that April morning
With its green maples of early summer
Yet the person waiting for you is still
The one who waited for you once in vain

I am here on a late night in November
Waiting for you under the parasol trees
The dull autumn rain talkatively
Beats upon my broken umbrella
Beats upon my heart that burns with anxiety

*"French parasol" is the Chinese name for the plane tree.

As heavily as rain falls from the sky
The rain in my heart falls more heavily
Autumn's night rain is gloomy and cold under the parasol trees
Yet the rain in my heart is warm
Without any goading, this heart of mine
Believes: Although you stood me up that early summer morning
In the night rain of late autumn you certainly will come

OCTOBER 1, 1980

In the Remote (Zai Yuanfang)

Eyes, My Eyes

Eyeache, dizziness: the comrade ophthalmologist
Said these are symptoms of "eye fatigue."

Eyes, my eyes,
You're tired, I owe you an apology.
I'm the one who gets you excessively tired,
The one who doesn't treasure you enough;
I won't let you close to build up energy,
Won't let you disinterestedly open and shut.
Eyes, my eyes,
You're tired, I owe you an apology.

Eyes, my eyes,
You're tired, this is a punishment for me.
To look at flowers in bright sunlight
Seems like looking into a colorful fog,
To look far away on happy days
Seems to blur my eyes with tears.
Eyes, my eyes,
You're tired, this is a punishment for me.

Eyes, my eyes,
You're tired, but I'm not to blame.
For, as you know, I never see enough
Of life in this world,
And although not a few things are ugly and evil,
The beautiful objects are far more numerous.
Eyes, my eyes,
You're tired, but I'm not to blame.

Eyes, my eyes,
You're tired, I don't believe you would betray me.
I bathed you clean with tears,
And together we walked from the nightmare back to a bright human
    world,
Under blue sky I counted my wife's gray hairs
And studied the grass-colored skirt of the vast earth.
Eyes, my eyes,
You're tired, I don't believe you would betray me.

Eyes, my eyes,
Help me distinguish—faces in the crowd.
Please don't let line upon line of words
Be transformed into misty curves of vapor;
Let my eyes once more see shining truth
And not page after page of murky lies.
Eyes, my eyes,
Help me smile back at thousands of faces smiling welcome.

MARCH 5, 1980

Lake Tian (Tian Chi)

SHAO YANXIANG   53

Lei Shuyan

(1942–) was born in Xi'an and, after more than ten years in the army, attended Northwest University. After graduation he was an editor of a literary magazine and now is employed by *Workers' Press,* a large newspaper with a circulation of ten million. He has published nine books of his poems and has received several awards, including a National Prize for Poetry for his book *The Small Grass Is Singing.* His poems have been translated into four continental European languages. He is a member of the Chinese Writers' Association.

Creation

With the scalpel of time
I cut mystic fissures in the brain.

All that has not yet happened
That has already happened
That will happen
Is rippling water within those fissures.

Where no beauty exists
I would create beauty.

I shall create a planet
And get it ready to collide with earth.

Three Hundred Lyric Poems by Modern Young Poets

Adoration

The Mountain:
    I am the foundation of mankind's sculpture.

The Sun:
    I am a golden apple in his hand,
    Pitched from the right into the left.

The Water:
    Now that I have seen the pure of heart,
    I am aware of my slime.

The Gorilla:
    The beauty of human beings
    Makes me too shy to leave the mountain forest.

The Star:
    With thousands of eyes I stare at earth
    For I envy mankind.

God:
    Gathering all manner of beauty into myself,
    I still feel inferior to man.

Time:
    Once man came on the scene,
    I could stop sleeping soundly.

The Sky:
    My interminable variations
    Imitate man's pleasure, anger, sorrow, and joy.

The Future:
    Only because man exists
    Do I.

Marble:
    Man
    Endowed me with beauty and life.

The Desert:
    My misery and ugliness
    Lie in my disdain for mankind.

The Universe:
    All the stars darkened in my bosom
    Are shining in man's hands.

Beauty:
    I am proud
    That I am the shadow of man.

        *   *   *

There is no hatred
No sexual urge
Nor heated debates.

O brilliant scientists,
You've created so perfect a "man"
As to completely eliminate shortcomings
That man himself cannot overcome.

No disease
No desire
No extraneous words
Neither doubt nor broken promises.

Without grief
Without creativity
It exists,
Exists just waiting for a command.

I am deeply grieved
At this simulation of human behavior—
Fake man!

AUGUST 1980

The Rhythm of the Sea (Hai Yun), no. 3 (March 1981)

In Pursuit

I'm not the water of the Yangtze River
But the yearning tears of the Snowy Mountains.
Drop by drop, day and night, they drip and flow
Then rush into the ocean that I long for.

Since my heart is betrothed to a distant place,
That's where my ideal is.
I'm not afraid of high mountains and isolated roads,
For I must seek my ocean.

I'm not afraid of zig-zags,
Falls and tumbles.
The pain of yearning
Lasts longer than the pain of seeking.

Bright sun, don't argue me into staying.
Steep cliffs, don't block my strides.
Betraying my ideal, accepting other situations
Would drive me stark mad.

Though I'm unsure which road leads there,
I know where the ideal resides.
Even if I have to make a thousand detours
And suffer a thousand setbacks, I will never lose heart.

Highlights of Chinese New Poetry: 1950-1980

Xu Gang

(1945-) was born in Shanghai and was drafted into the army in 1962. He began publishing poetry in 1963 and became famous during the Cultural Revolution for his poems in support of the regime in power. In 1974 he was graduated from Beijing University. He worked for *The People's Daily*, China's most important newspaper, for a number of years until 1987. Published collections of his poetry include *The Great River of Full Tide, The Flower of Rain, Dedicated to October, Songs for the Far Away*, and *One Hundred Lyrics*. He has received the National Prize for Poetry, the *October Magazine* Award, the Yu Hua Prize, and other awards. His outlook and writing style have changed considerably since his career as a writer began. He lived in Guangdong Province in 1989 and has since lived in Paris.

Red Azalea on the Cliff

Red azalea, smiling
From the cliffside at me,
You make my heart shudder with fear!
A body could smash and bones splinter in the canyon—
Beauty, always looking on at disaster.

But red azalea on the cliff,
That you comb your twigs even in a mountain gale
Calms me down a bit.
Of course you're not wilfully courting danger,
Nor are you at ease with whatever happens to you.
You're merely telling me: beauty is nature.

Would anyone like to pick a flower
To give to his love
Or pin to his own lapel?
On the cliff there is no road
And no azalea grows where there is a road.
If someone actually reached that azalea,
Then an azalea would surely bloom in his heart.

Red azalea on the cliff,
You smile like the Yellow Mountains,
Whose sweetness encloses slyness,
Whose intimacy embraces distance.
You remind us all of our first love.
Sometimes the past years look
Just like the azalea on the cliff.

MAY 1982
Yellow Mountain
Revised at Hangzhou

Three Hundred Lyric Poems by Modern Young Poets

The Northern Mountain

Now there's a mountain to remember!
Nothing pretty or magnificent
But simple as yellow loess.
The reproaches it has borne for bleakness
Go as far back as time.

I lean upon a chaotic heap of stones.
My heart is so close to them
That it feels their warmth.
No words here, just an expanse of waving grass
Blown by winds from the empty valley.
I have picked out a fragment that history lost.

This, the Northern Mountain, once had
Splendid peaks and ridges too sublime for words.
Flowers, trees, and songbirds used to thrive there;
So did a clear spring that people said was holy.
Incense smoke curled up inside a Buddhist temple.

The forest has plenty of axes and clubs,
The loggers' rudeness enshrouds the mountain.
Tall trees and short ones
Fall down one after another.
Having lost this protective screen,
The low grass and the wellspring
Die away in grief.

Why not chase away the axes and clubs?
Since ancient times, we have found it hardest
To deprive ourselves of cutting tools
And reasons for cutting.
"When there shall be no more tree cutting"—
That is the green fantasy of the deserted mountain,
A dream so long and simple . . .

The Tide of Poetry (Shichao), no. 1 (January 1985)

Summer

Only hot pursuit can ripen
This green olive called summer.
Astringent, beery, a bubble . . .
It splashes swimsuits of every
Color up and down the beach.
The cross goes into exile
Once the heart is exposed,
Too impatient to wait for fall picking,
Salted bitter with seawater.

Poetry Magazine (Shikan), no. 8 (August 1986)

A Figure Seen from Behind

I can see only your back
As you stand facing the mountain.
Watching your excitement before that height,
I would prefer to hide my name in a cave
Like an outlaw taking to the greenwood.
Sometimes climbing is a way of sinking,
And sinking a way of climbing.
The ancient cave is prolonged, and deep,
I'm setting out from the eyes toward the mind.

Poetry Magazine (Shikan), no. 8 (August 1986)

Cigarette Butts

My cigarette butts are my forest,
I'm piously addicted to the drug;
Without a smoke I get too lonely,
I love the fire, love the bright glow.
On a gloomy sunless day,
The fire in me never dies out.
That's how my imagination takes wing.
Nobody escapes the day of burial.
I want to be buried here in my forest.

Poetry Magazine (Shikan), no. 8 (August 1986)

Ye Yanbing

(1948-) has recently been editor of the poetry magazine *Stars*. A member of the Chinese Writers' Association, he was recently awarded a National Prize for Poetry. One of his books is entitled *Duet: Selected Poems*.

Tracking Rope

1

My destiny
runs a short way
from my shoulder to the boat

From a young heart clenched like a fist
a contracted tendon
I pass life
into the heavy aged boat

The moment the boat gets its life
I get mine
—with a bloody shoulder

2

I once had a childhood—
green illusions
and the sun's fraternal caresses

When I grew energetic and strong
I left the warm fragrant fields

A gray-haired mother
with cracked hands
rubbed and kneaded me

Her son would track boats against the current
I was her ceaseless yearning

3

Straighten the curved riverbed
Curve straight backbones
I am the boatmen's low guttural song—
that leaden melody

A path was built for me on perilous cliffs
A village appeared before me on the canal
I am the horizon of history
the mother's dusk and the son's morning

4

I belong to the boat
to its stamina for carrying a heavy load
but not to its heavy inertia

The boat abuses me
for my stubbornness that deprives it of peace

I belong to the boat
I belong even more to the tracker's will power
that strikes like a whip against heavy inertia

5

I am tired and want to rest
I want to fade into the steady snore of the tracker

But again the great river nudges and wakens a new voyage
again Venus beckons the first rays of morning sun
again the gorge ekes out a path
and again dewdrops moisten footprints

Then the tracker and I together
haul a sopping-wet morning once again

OCTOBER 1981

Selected Poetry of 1981

The Circular Expressway and Straight Lines of the Ancient City

To Beijing's First Grade-separated Expressway

This city that died yesterday
Consists of numerous squares—
Square mahjong tiles on square tables in the teahouses,
Each square gray brick in the foundations of the imperial palace,
Every crowded compound a quadrangle off a narrow lane,
The concubines' forbidden garden behind the Forbidden City—
These ossified strips and frames
The distinctive features of the ancient city.

We're face to face with the dead heritage left by the past
In numerous crisscrossing straight lines,
A stoplight hanging high above each intersection.

With frequent sudden stops at high speed
And many delays during rush hour,
Dead history erects an invisible,
Yet dignified, fence around the living city!

So I salute the first grade-separated expressway
As it appears like a huge circular full stop
To punctuate a city squared off like gridded stationery.

Finished! The stiff, dull, slow characters
Written by numerous houses. At intersections
Of the grade-separated expressway, the wind
Of rolling wheels brings new language from this highway
Like the fission of atoms in an accelerator,
Bombarding the conservative and complacent
Who have not become corpses in those ossified structures
That have occupied this ancient city for hundreds of years.

Highlights of Chinese New Poetry: 1950–1980

I Sing the Harvest

1

The harvest is an ancient ballad
Perhaps the first that human beings ever had

Ancient Greeks wild-eyed in eulogy of Bacchus
Rapture kindled the women's blonde hair
People of the East carry white oxtail and sing eight songs
The pupils of their dark eyes ripen with love
Because human beings with sincere hearts have won the harvest
They have escaped the vulture shadow of starvation
So that symphonies of colors and voices come forth
In early morning on the five-line staff of cooking smoke

Extracting harvests from dark oily ground
Extricating mankind from a world of carnivores and blood drinkers!

2

I am not a romantic poet
Who compares sowing to a god dispensing happiness

Fire burning fallow grass roasts the last of winter
Melts the frozen crystal arch of the sky
Let the red hot sunbeams spurt down
To enamel in reddish bronze the people pulling ploughs
Every blue vein resembles a bent bow
Shooting jets of hope into furrows spanning the fields
Ploughed ridges incubate compacted lives
And pearls of sweat engender the greening dream

Thus human beings pull this heavy planet earth
Sowing life into this still universe . . .

3

"Plant melon, harvest melon; plant beans, harvest beans"—
But stand in a field that is not yours
And the harvest is merely the sower's tragedy!

Clearly the anemic earth is no longer pregnant
But people still beg stingy heaven for charity
Clearly awakened life no longer cares to be duped
Yet people still curse their betrayal by innocent fate
"The poet who stole language that angered god"
Was brought by the world before an inquisition

"Sow dragon's teeth and harvest fleas"—
Sow seeds of truth in fields that want to sleep
And the rocks of stupidity break the shiny plough!

4

I raise both my arms to laud the fierce summer
The harvest is a sailor climbing on deck in a storm

Our ancestors beat a thunderous drum
Green soldiers leaped into a green war
Springing into wilderness, desert, and rocky crevices
Declaring an occupation with their unconquerable presence
Through green leaves declaring the right to bathe in light
Declaring with budding flowers the right to quench love's thirst
Each seed soaked in hot sweat
Manifests the sower's fearless spirit

Unless summer baptizes with its thunderstorm
The harvest stays puny and never becomes a giant!

5

I too am a green warrior—
The long summer has cast me
In a field my motherland ploughed for me

The hot wind parches the veins of fantasy
I stretch roots down toward moist layers of earth
Ruthless lightning truncates the body of faith
I suck out calcium from the unselfish earth
A cruel thunderstorm attacks the buds of love's flowers
I ferment honey in this vast warm land

I too am a green warrior—
Green cell in a green leaf of my motherland's
Nine million six hundred thousand square kilometers.

6

The bumper crop belongs to the sowers
And harvest is just a prelude to new sowing

Seeds leave their boughs in order to return to earth
People reap from the earth in order to plough her
Like the seed of fire passed down from Olympus
Like a short furlough between two campaigns
Yes, this is our incomparable joy
To bestow the sower's chromosomes
Swaddled in earth's womb
Upon babies that come yelling and screaming into the world

The harvest is an ancient ballad—
Every seed is her youthful singer!

NOVEMBER 1981
Beijing

Huacheng Poetry Supplement (Huacheng Shige Zengkan), ca. 1985

74   YE YANBING

Bei Dao

is the pen name of Zhao Zhenkai (1949–), who was born in Beijing. During the 1960s he was educated in a prestigious secondary school and became a member of the Red Guard movement. He began writing poetry in 1970 during an eleven-year period of manual labor which included working in an iron foundry. As cofounder of the unofficial typescript magazine *Today* (Jintian), he became the best-known figure of the controversial young group known as "obscurist poets" because of the alleged ambiguity in their work. Their poems expressed personal feelings, including melancholy and depression, which authorities had banned as a threat to public morale.

Although *Today* was eventually suppressed, its writers enjoyed a favorable press and relatively mild censure from the government, which eventually loosened its controls over their publication. Approved magazines began to publish work by the risk-taking authors of *Today,* none of whom had been known before the Cultural Revolution (1967–76). Bei Dao became a culture hero for educated youth who saw their own personal scepticism, suspicions, and griefs reflected in his poetry and fiction.

In the early and mid–1980s, Bei Dao's poems appeared in many Chinese mainstream publications. As an editor employed by the Foreign Language Bureau in Beijing, he worked on the Esperanto edition of the *Beijing Review*. In 1986 he had a short-lived job as poetry editor of the controversial monthly *China* until it was forcibly taken over by officials of the Chinese Writers' Association. After the government's reaction to the student demonstrations for "bourgeois liberalism" in late 1986, Bei Dao became unemployable and his work —like that of most other obscurist poets—could not be published in China. In 1987, he accepted a one-year position as a visiting scholar at Durham University in England. His wife, the painter Shao Fei, and their child joined him there. In the fall of 1988 he was writer in residence at the University of Iowa and gave readings on a tour of several American cities. He spent the early part of 1989 in the United States and has since resided with his family on the European continent.

Bei Dao's poetry is sometimes tranquil but rarely happy. He has said that in poetry he uses common techniques of film montage —juxtaposed images and changes in speed—that he hopes will arouse the reader's imagination to fill in substantial gaps between the words. His book *Collected Poems (Shi Xuan)* was published in 1985, and a second, expanded edition was issued in 1987 by New Century Publishing Company in Guangdong. Poems of his were also published in *Selected Poems by Bei Dao and Gu Cheng* (Stockholm, 1983), and his translations into Chinese have appeared in *Selected Modern Poetry of Northern Europe.* Successive collections of his poems have been translated into English by Bonnie S. McDougall under the titles *Notes from the City of the Sun: Poems By Bei Dao* (Ithaca, N.Y.: Cornell University East Asia Papers, 1983) and *The August Sleepwalker* (London: Anvil Press Poetry, 1988; New York: New Directions Publishing, 1990).

Chords

The grove and I closely
Encircle the small lake
A hand plunges into the water
Rousing swifts from a deep sleep
The wind is all alone
The sea is much too far away

When I walk out on city streets
The traffic clangor stops behind a red light
Shadows open like a fan
Footprints twist crookedly
The safety island is all alone
The sea is much too far away

Downstairs a blue window
Illumines a group of boys
Who strum a guitar and hum a tune
The ends of their cigarettes glow and fade
The stray cat is all alone
The sea is much too far away

When you fall asleep on the beach
The wind pulls up short at your mouth
Waves stealthily lap nearby
Shaped in soft curves
The dream is all alone
The sea is much too far away

Three Hundred Lyric Poems by Modern Young Poets

Bodhisattva

The robe's sinuous billowing
Reveals your gentle breathing

Myriad eyes have opened wide
On the thousand palms of your swaying hands
As they caress an electrified stillness
And make all earthly things crisscross and overlap
Just as in a dream
You sit crosslegged on a lotus in full bloom
Pleasure has its roots in the soil

You are enduring a hundred-year thirst
The pearl inlaid in your forehead
Epitomizes the mighty ocean's invincible power
To make a grain of sand transparent
As water

However clearheadedly you face the day
You seem to have drifted into a sound sleep

You show no differentiation of sex
Half naked breasts protrude
Because you only want to be a mother
To nurture the griefs of all living creatures
To raise them to maturity

Three Hundred Lyric Poems by Modern Young Poets

Declaration

For the martyr Yu Luoke*

Perhaps the last moment is here
I haven't left a will
Only a pen . . . to my mother
I'm not a hero
In an era without heroes
I just wanted to be a man

The quiet horizon
Separated the ranks of the living from the dead
I had to choose the sky
And would never kneel on the ground
To let executioners look gigantic
So they could block the wind of freedom

Out of starlike bullet holes
A bloody dawn is flowing

Today (Jintian), no. 8 (February 1980)

*Yu Luoke was a young writer accused of violating socialist policy when he argued
that social class is not necessarily inherited. He was executed in 1970, about six years
before the end of the Cultural Revolution.

Rainy Night

When night broken in a reflecting puddle
Swayed the new leaf
As if rocking its infant to sleep
When lamplight strung raindrops together
And made decorations over your shoulders
Twinkling and then falling to the ground
You said no
In a most resolute tone
Yet your smile divulged the secret in your heart

The wet palms of low dark clouds
Stroked your hair with the fragrance of flowers
And my boiling hot breath
People's shadows lengthened under street lamps
Merging every intersection, merging every dream
Catching our cheerful riddles in a net
Tears cemented with bitterness
Moisten your handkerchief
Forgotten in a pitch-dark gateway

If even by tomorrow morning
The gun muzzle and bloody clouds of dawn
Force me to give up freedom, youth, and pen
I will never give up this evening
I will never give you up
Let walls barricade my mouth
Let iron bars partition my sky
A tide of blood will go on as long as my heart beats
Your smile will be engraved on the scarlet moon
As it rises each night at my small window
To awaken all my memories

1976

Today (Jintian), no. 4 (June 20, 1979)

Ancient Temple

The dying sound of a bell
Knits a spider web, spreading into annual ringing
Circle after circle of crevices in the wood column
The stones have no memory
Stones that once launched echoes in the hazy valley
Have no memory
When the path made a detour away from here
Dragons and monstrous birds also flew away
Lifting the hoarse bells right off the eaves
Along with unrecorded legends
The inscriptions on the wall have become so weathered
That only in a huge conflagration
Would they be made recognizable
Wild grass grows there
Once a year, so indifferent
It doesn't care whether the owners it submits to
Are the cloth shoes of the monks
Or just the wind
Fragmentary tombstones support the sky
Perhaps in response to a living person's sight
The tortoise might be resurrected
With a heavy secret on its back
And creep across the threshold

Shanghai Literature (Shanghai Wenxue), no. 5 (May 1981)

An Artist's Life

Go buy a radish
—Mother said
Hey, don't cross the median stripe
—The cop said
O magnificent Sea, where are you
—A drunkard said

Why have all the street lights exploded
—I said
A blind man passing by
Deftly raised a bamboo cane
As if thrusting up an antenna
A shrieking ambulance pulled up close
Took me to the hospital

And that's how I became a model patient
Sneezing in roars
Counting with my eyes closed the seconds till mealtime
Once again I donated blood to bedbugs
No time for sighing
Finally I too became a doctor
A big syringe with a thick needle in hand
I paced the corridor
To kill time all night long

Collected Poems, 2nd ed.

Resumé

I once strutted goosestep across the square
The hair of my head shaved clean to the roots
In order to more readily find the sun
Nevertheless in that crazy season
Turned in a contrary direction, separated by fences
I met with those deadpan goats
Until I beheld the ideal on a sheet
Of white paper that looked like saline-alkaline soil
I arched my back thinking
I had found the only medium fit
For expressing the truth, like a fish who,
While being baked, dreams about the sea
Viva! I let out just one fucking yell
Before my whiskers sprouted
Tangled like the uncounted centuries
I had no choice but to battle history
And use knives to make those idols
My kinsfolk, but it was no way to cope
With a world split up from a fly's eyes
Surrounded by piles of books that endlessly wrangle
We peacefully divvied up the small change
We had made by selling off every star
In one night I gambled away everything
Down to my waistbelt, coming back to earth again naked

A quietly lit cigarette
Is a fatal shot at that midnight
When the sky and the earth changed places
I was hanging upside down
In an old tree that looked like a swabbing mop
I gazed far off into the distance

Collected Poems, 2nd ed.

Temptation

As long as the world lasts
One kind of temptation won't change
It makes who knows how many sailors lose their lives
The stone dam prevents
The tilted continent from sliding to the ocean floor

Dolphins leap over the constellation
And fall down, the white sandy beach
Vanishes in dissolving moonlight
The sea tide crosses the stone dam
And comes across the empty square
Beached octopuses hang from every lamppost
Sea water rises above the house steps
Gushes in through doors and windows
Chases people watching the sea in their dreams

Poetry Magazine (Shikan), no. 6 (June 1981)

Electric Shock

A shapeless person I once met
Shook hands, a painful scream
My hand was burned
And left with scars
Whenever I meet people with a shape
And shake hands, a painful scream
Their hands are burned
And left with scars
I dare not shake hands with people anymore
And I always hide my hands behind my back
But when I pray
To heaven, I clasp my hands
A painful scream
The deepest place in my heart
Is left with scars

Poetry Magazine (Shikan), no. 6 (June 1981)

The Single Room

When he was born the furniture looked massive and stately
Now it looks squat and meager and worn
With no doors or windows, the only light source is a bulb
He's satisfied with the room temperature
But curses out loud at that invisible nasty weather
Liquor bottles full of hatred are lined up in one corner
Their caps removed, who knows who's been drinking with whom
He's frantically hammering nails into the walls
So imaginary crippled horses can leap those hurdles

A slipper in pursuit of bedbugs stomps
The ceiling, leaving the flowery print of an ideal
He thirsts to see blood
His own blood, splash like rays of morning sun

Poetry Magazine (Shikan), no. 6 (June 1981)

A Dream of the Harbor

As layers of moonlight rush into the harbor
This night appears translucent
The smooth-worn steps one above the other
Are leading to the sky
Leading to a world in my dreams

I'm back in my home town
Bringing coral and salt to my mother
The coral grows into a forest
The salt melts a glacier
A girl's eyelashes
Shake down ripened grains of wheat
The wet wind blows past
The cliff's aging forehead
My love song
Comes to visit at every window
Beer foam spills over into the streets
And changes into street lights
I walk toward the skyline
Rimmed with reddish beams of the setting sun
Then I turn back
To make a long deep bow

The wave's crest brushes the decks and the sky
The star looks into the compass
For its own daytime position
No, I'm not a sailor
Just a born landlubber
But I've hung my heart like an anchor
    On the ship's gunwale
And go out to sea now with my pals

Huacheng Poetry Supplement (Huacheng Shige Zengkan), ca. 1985

Gao Falin

(1950–) is a graduate of Wuhan University and a member of the Chinese Writers' Association. He has published three collections of poetry and has been awarded the National Prize for Poetry.

Iron Meteorite

An iron meteorite is on display in Beijing Planetarium.

I said:

Once brilliant orb, who left nothing but this remnant,
You mishap of an early death caused by impatience.

How disciplined your companions are
To hold their assigned courses, never moving an inch away.

You exchanged humility and trepidation for enduring peace
And have earned the right to shine cowardly forever.

You alone—stubborn son of a planet—
Furiously ran amuck and so burned to ashes.

You said:

I hate soul-suffocating darkness,
Likewise the hope that life is eternally pallid!

I wanted to search the mighty universe
For bright green forests and pure clouds!

Though dying, I whipped along on the back of night
And darkness, like dead water, divided and rejoined!

You see, I was carefree all the while I burned;
My demise proves my existence.

Three Hundred Lyric Poems by Modern Young Poets

Random Thoughts While Skating

A

Musical notes moving gracefully
Fast handwriting that sways freely
The wind's song
The madcap dance of light
Sketch of a cloud
Water sculpture
Are alloyed into one substance

B

In a pure white universe
Red-orange and bright blue comets turn back toward earth
Which has lost its gravity
The atmosphere can't stop them

How fine! Unhampered and unconfined!
Although the orbits behind us overlap
Everyone feels a happy loneliness
In those moments of rushing forward

C

Ice, ice, even at your coldest
You can't freeze sharp skates after all
I dash over the bitterly cold ice
And use the power and speed of my youth
To let it melt under my feet
If only for just a split second
Then it turns back into what it was before

D

No matter how far you skate
No matter how confused these arcs and circles get
There must be a line that slightly yet clearly
Joins the present coordinates and the starting point
I don't elude history
History has crystalized
Yet no life will ever be repeated

Three Hundred Lyric Poems by Modern Young Poets

Flint

I am flint
I have angular edges and corners

I'm not so gorgeous as diamonds and emeralds
Nor elegant as white marble and green jade
I've never been carved into an imperial seal
That feudal lords would risk their lives to seize
Modern women don't think me worth wearing on their tender
    fingers
Or hanging around their milky necks
I can't compete with sliding glaciers and gravel
In being a heavyweight subject for geological treatises

I am flint
I make just one request
Please pick me up
—Strike

Yes   strike me very hard!
In a flash I can open like a gray cocoon
As the colorful light of life bursts from my soul's depths
Strike me and by striking prove that I
Am not mere wasted detritus even though
I've slept in a marsh or valley for ten thousand years
For I am a point of crystalized fire
Silent star
Hardened flower

Strike me and by striking know how the past reappears
Radiant as clouds of dawn in a dream
Not until man discovered me
Could he build civilization out of empty wilderness
From cuneiform to pyramid
From pottery and the rise of Buddhism
To the horses painted by Xu Beihong*

I am flint
Please be mindful of my experience
The fire of wisdom did not fly down from outside the world
From the beginning it is buried beneath your feet or his or hers

The Contemporary Age (Dang Dai), no. 4 (April 1981)

*Xu Beihong was a Chinese painter famous for his skillful pictures of horses.

Zhao Lihong

(1950–) was born and educated in Shanghai. He began writing poetry and artistic prose in high school, graduating in 1968, and was afterward assigned to farming in his father's native home, Chong Ming, an island close to Shanghai. He struggled to make a scanty living while continuing to write. After the Cultural Revolution, he studied Chinese literature at East China Normal University and soon became a nationally known poet. His works have appeared in many magazines and he has published about ten books, including collections of poetry entitled *Venus by the Sea, The Grass of Life,* and *The Soul of Poetry.* He has been deputy chief editor of *Buds Monthly (Meng Ya)* and recently was granted the title of professional writer by the Chinese Writers' Association. He is also a member of the Chinese Prose Writers' Society.

Reverie beside an Old Bed of the Yellow River

Was this bed once churned by the Yellow River?
Why can't I hear the thunder of its tide,
Or see its muddy waves lapping the sky?
A line of wild reeds and some clumps of wormwood
Are bathed instead by forlorn autumn winds
Telling their old stories of desolation.

Ask those rocks scattered across the wide basin
How the Yellow River swaggered through here
For years like a naive, rash blusterer
Who shouted, shoved, bounced, elbowed through each valley
Hoping it would lead out to the vast ocean
And every plain extend to remote goals . . .
He was fooled and got lost in this flat country.
Ah, impetuous young Yellow River,
How you meandered one way then another.
How tentatively grief poured from your heart
How terribly you sobbed for the distant ocean.

Now the river runs a different course
Toward the ocean, and the world it describes
Belongs to heroes who, despite all setbacks,
Advance into the very prime of life
That the old river must not have forgotten.
Look at those boulders thrown from cloud-rimmed mountains,
Look at this tenuous, parched riverbed,
Where the amazing boot tracks still remain
From his perilous thrusts and explorations.

As I stand and think about this land
I hear the ancient singing of the River
I hear his obstinate, indomitable
Step still echoing far ahead of me.

AUTUMN 1982

Stars (Xing Xing), no. 3 (March 1983)

A Fragrant Osmanthus Tree Planted in the Song Dynasty

We met by chance
In this unfrequented ancient garden
And we stand talking to each other
Tonight in the autumn drizzle

I speak by staring
Voiceless questions
And offer you quiet solace
From root to crown

You speak with vitalizing fragrance
Whose candid eloquence
Waters the field of my heart
Now and again . . .

You've stood for a thousand years
Blossoming gorgeously a thousand times
A thousand times silently predicting
Autumns of red oranges and yellow shaddock
Though heaven and earth turn upside down
Your language never changes
But goes on fragrant as ever, always sweet-scented . . .

Together then
In our own languages
Let's steadfastly
Pour out our deepest belief

Selected Lyrics of Contemporary China

The Pledge

What is carved into rock
Is perhaps not imperishable
What gets printed
Isn't necessarily immortal

Things floating away like hazy smoke
Are not absolutely doomed to vanish
The shooting star that plummets
Will not necessarily disappear

A sincere smile
And a glance like unheard lightning
Coming from the heart
Are far better
Than a solemn vow of love
That sounds like a thunderbolt

OCTOBER 1982

Stars (Xing Xing), no. 3 (March 1983)

Shu Ting

(1952-) was born in Fujian Province and, when still a child, she was sent to the countryside after her father was accused of being a rightist. Intellectual relatives stimulated her interest in literature and she read foreign literary works at an early age. The Cultural Revolution interrupted her junior high school education. In 1969 she was sent to western Fujian, returning to Xiamen in 1972. After a period of unemployment she held many odd jobs, including work in textile and light bulb factories. She became associated with the editors and authors of *Today (Jintian),* and is now a well-known poet and member of the Chinese Writers' Association. In the mid-1980s she was honored with membership on the association's board. She has worked as a correspondent for the *Beijing Review.* Two collections of her poetry, *Selected Poems by Shu Ting and Gu Cheng* and *Two-Masted Ship,* were published in 1982. Her poems have been translated into ten languages, and she has traveled extensively in Europe, India, and the United States.

To Mother

Your pale fingers combing the hair at my temples,
I can't help holding tight to the front of your coat
    Just as I did when I was little.
Oh Mother,
To keep intact the gradually fading shadow of your figure,
Though dawn's first light scissored my dream to wisps of smoke
I still dared not open my eyes for a long time.

I still cherish your bright red scarf,
Yet am always afraid that washing may take away
    Your special warm fragrance.
Oh Mother,
Isn't the current of time just that ruthless?
How can I dare open the painted screen of memory
When I am afraid that its colors might likewise fade.

I once came crying to you with a splinter,
Now wearing a crown of thorns, I dare not
    Groan even once.
Oh Mother,
How often I look up sadly at your picture.
Even if my cry could pierce that clay soil,
How could I dare to bother your peaceful rest?

I still dare not display gifts of love like this,
Even though I have written many songs
    To flowers, to the sea, to daybreak.
Oh Mother,
These sweet abiding memories I hold dear
Are neither swift current nor waterfall, but an ancient well
Overgrown with flowering shrubs and out of voice for singing.

AUGUST 1, 1975

Today (Jintian), no. 1 (December 1978)

100   SHU TING

Two-Masted Ship

Fog moistens both wings
But the wind allows no dallying
O shore, beloved shore
We parted just yesterday
And you are here again today
Tomorrow at a different latitude
We shall meet along my course

Remember the storm, the lighthouse
That brought us together
Another storm, a different light
Drove us asunder again
Even though morning or evening
Sky and ocean stand between us
You are always on my voyage
I am always in your sight

AUGUST 27, 1979

Shanghai Literature (Shanghai Wenxue), no. 2 (February 1980)

To the Oak Tree

If I love you—
I never behave like a climbing trumpet vine
Using your high branches to show myself off;
If I love you—
I never mimic infatuated little birds
Repeating monotonous songs into the shadows,
Nor do I look at all like a wellspring
Sending out its cooling consolation all year round,
Or just another perilous crag
Augmenting your height, setting off your prestige.
Nor like the sunlight
Or even spring rain.
No, these are not enough.
I would be a kapok tree by your side
Standing with you—both of us shaped like trees.
Our roots hold hands underground,
Our leaves touch in the clouds.
As a gust of wind passes by
We salute each other
And not a soul
Understands our language.
You have your bronze boughs and iron trunk
Like knives and swords,
Also like halberds;
I have my red flowers
Like heavy sighs,
Also like heroic torches.
We share cold waves, storms and thunderbolts;
Together we savor fog, haze and rainbows.
We seem to always live apart,
But actually depend upon each other forever.

This has to be called extraordinary love.
Faith resides in it:
Love—
I love not only your sublime body
But the space you occupy,
The land beneath your feet.

MARCH 27, 1977

Poetry Magazine (Shikan), no. 5 (May 1982)

Farewell in the Rain

I wanted to throw open the car door, rush to you
And cry out upon your broad shoulders:
"I can't restrain myself—I really can't!"
I wanted to clasp your hand, flee together
Toward the recently cleared sky and the fields
Without faltering, without glancing back.

I wish I could have garnered all my soft feelings
And had them awaken you at last
With an eye incapable of pleading.

I wanted, really wanted. . .
My suffering turns into such melancholy I can't
Get past it, can't dredge it up into words.

APRIL 1977

Literature and Arts of the Ocean (Haiyang Wenyi), no. 3 (March 1979)

Uneasy Night in a Hotel

The love announcement co-authored by lip prints and a tear
Bravely climbs up the pillar into the postbox
Which is ice cold
And has been out of commission a long time
The paper strip sealing it like a bandage wavers faintly in the wind

The eaves curve softly under a black cat's paws
Large trucks ride over sleep till it's flattened thin and hard
Sprinters
Dream all night long of the starting pistol's shot
The jugglers can't hold onto their eggs
Street lamps explode with a screech
Paint the color of egg yolk makes night seem all the more scraggly

A woman in a nightgown
Opens the door like an earthquake
Bare feet dash like crazy deer across the carpet
A huge flying moth flutters across the wall
Flames spurt out above the jangling telephone

The receiver sounds completely
Silent
Only snow
Sings unceasingly on the electric wire far away

Fuzhou
NOVEMBER 30, 1986

Wen Hui Monthly (Wenhui Yuekan), no. 3 (March 1988)

A Self-Portrait

She's his little schemer.

When begged for an answer, she keeps quiet,
When silence is needed, she laughs and makes jokes
Causing him all sorts of razzle-dazzle.
She upsets equilibrium,
She looks down on conceptualizing,
She dances weird steps around him
Like a wilful little wood demon.

She's his little schemer.

What he dreams of, she won't give,
What he never expected, she compels him to take.
Though drawn by tenderness, she avoids expressing it,
Though she hasn't gotten any, she's already afraid of losing it.
A whirlpool herself,
She creates various other whirlpools.
Nobody understands her magic.

She's his little schemer.

Beckoned, she won't come; waved away, she stays;
Seeming close, she's far off; he'd give up, but can't.
One time she seems like an iceberg,
Another time like a fiery ocean,
Sometimes she's a wordless song.
While listening, he thinks it may be true or false;
After tasting, he can't tell whether it's sweet or hot.

His, his,
She's his little schemer.

Fujian Literature (Fujian Wenxue), no. 7 (July 1980)

O Motherland, Dear Motherland

I am the old broken waterwheel beside your river
That has composed a centuries-old song of weariness;
I'm the smoke-smudged miner's lamp on your forehead
That lights your snail-like crawl through the cave of history.
I'm the withered rice-ear, the washed-out roadbed,
The barge mired in a silt shoal
As the tow rope cuts
Deeply into your shoulder
—O Motherland.

I am poverty,
I'm sorrow,
I'm the bitterly painful hope
Of your generations.
I am the flowers strewn from Apsara's* flowing sleeves
That after thousands of years still have not reached earth
—O Motherland.

I am your untarnished ideal
Just broken away from the cobweb of myths;
I'm a bud of the ancient lotus** blanketed under your snow,
I'm your smiling dimple wet with tears;
Your newly drawn lime-white starting line.
I'm the scarlet dawn emerging with long shimmering rays
—O Motherland.

*Flying Apsaras entertained the Buddhas with music and are portrayed in the frescoes of the Dunhuang Caves.

**This lotus is said to have sprung from a seed that was planted after being kept in an airless tomb for two thousand years.

I am numbered among your billions,
The sum of your nine million square kilometers.
You with the scar-blemished breast
Have nurtured me,
Me the confused, the ponderer, the seething,
So that from my body of flesh and blood
You might eke out
Your prosperity, your glory, and your freedom
—O Motherland,
My dear Motherland.

APRIL 20, 1979

Poetry Magazine (Shikan), no. 7 (July 1979)

Montages in Twilight

1

Sunlight diffuses thinly upon the low wall,
This summer is still cold.

2

Voice blurred with tears,
An alto takes pains to melt dusk
Into a puddle of syrup.

Let all those sticky wings
Fly unsteadily away.

3

Those whose flowers have withered once
Are the first to know what spring means;
Those who have never borne flowers
Think soonest of withering.

4

A horsetail pine begs the wind
To give him back his true shape.
The wind keeps on mocking him,
So he gets angrier
But still can't stop shaking.

5

None of those birds that flew up and away
Singing in the morning can return.
Lonely in late dusk, the groves of trees
Hang one curtain of sorrow after another.

6

The dusk and I must have a tacit agreement,
She often pauses, waits outside my window:
You'd have me send forth something? To whom?
There must be
                some secret I no longer remember.
She shakes her head,
Then walks away.

7

Loitering shadow,
Have you again extended your sucking disks?

8

Moonlight strives to tangle soft fronds of palm trees,
Then wilfully releases them again;
Stars flicked into thickets of grass
Crawl out with furtive smiles.

Vibrating footsteps signal someone walking,
So the sunflowers stop guessing at riddles.
Someone says: "I think I heard something."
The wind covers its mouth and follows after:
It's really not so strange. It's not!

9

If those thoughts cheeping in the crowded chicken coop
Were set free—
How far could they actually fly?

Faces behind the latticed window;
A soul behind its eyes;
Virgin forests behind that soul;
The eight-toned bird
Already knows it must not make a sound.

Something in the dark has to become visible.
All those things that do become visible
Are what people call the stars.

AUGUST–OCTOBER, 1981

Huacheng Poetry Supplement (Huacheng Shige Zengkan), ca. 1985

The Mirror

In the dark blue night
The old wounds burst open all at once
When the bed starts broiling these past events
It is a very patient lover
The table clock goes di da di da
And beats the dream black and blue all over its body
Groping along the wall
Groping along the wall for the light's pull-chain
I inadvertantly became entangled
With a thread of moonlight
Flashing silverfish smelled the scent and ascended on a root
And so finally
You are a pool of softness

With a slow turn of body
    You are looking at yourself
    Yes you are looking at your self

The full-length mirror feigns innocent indulgence in unrequited love
The ambiguous wallpaper blurs its patterns
And is framed solidly
Watching you yourself wither one petal after another
    You have no way to escape no way to escape
Even if you could jump over the walls one at a time
There are still days blocking your back that you cannot jump over.

Women don't need philosophy
Women can shake off the stains of the moon
The way a dog shakes off water

Draw the thick curtain closed
The dawn's moist tongue touches the window glass
Place yourself back
Into the concave indentation of the pillow
Like a loose roll of photographic negatives

All at once the walnut tree under the window shivers
As if caressed by an ice-cold hand.

Wen Hui Monthly (Wenhui Yuekan), no. 3 (March 1988)

Xu Demin

(1953–) was born in Shanghai and, after graduation from high school, went to the countryside in Jiangxi Province to do farm work. He attended the Professional School of Industrial Economy in Zhejiang Province, where he was assigned to a factory. In 1979 he was admitted to Fudan University and majored in economics. He published work in student journals and twice was the vice-chairman of the Student Association at Fudan University.

In 1981 he founded the Fudan Poetry Association and was its first chairman and the chief editor of its magazine, *Poetry Ploughs the Fields*. In 1982 he participated in the Youth Poetry Conference, sponsored by the Chinese Writers' Association and *Poetry Magazine*. His poem "A Young Watch Repairman" was awarded *Poetry Magazine*'s annual Excellent Work Award for 1982, and in the following year he joined the Shanghai Branch of the Chinese Writers' Association. Upon graduation from Fudan in 1983, he was retained by the university as a faculty member teaching political economy. He edited China's first college poetry anthology, *Sea Star* (Shanghai: Fudan University Press, 1984). In 1984 he joined a tour of the north organized by *Poetry Magazine*, and a group of his poems entitled "Purple Starfish" won both the *Shanghai Literature* Excellent Work Award and the Literature Award of Shanghai.

On sabbatical in 1986, he lived among working people in the northwestern provinces and wrote a novel entitled *How About It?* At year's end, the Shanghai Writers' Association sponsored a conference on his poetry. In 1987 he edited the *Shanghai Culture Annual* and directed Shanghai's first Artistic Culture Photography Competition.

Xu Demin has published over four hundred poems, short stories, novellas, reportage pieces, and articles on poetry and photography. A painter whose work has been exhibited in the Fine Arts Gallery of Shanghai, he has had eighty pieces of graphic art and photography published. His poems have appeared in thirty anthologies, including *Great Collection of China's Literature and Art: Poetry, Dictionary of New Poetry Appreciation, The Anthology of Young Poets*, and *The*

Anthology of Exploration Poetry. His collections of poems are *There Is Only One Tree Left to Time* (Shanghai: Shanghai Literature and Art Press, 1989), *Humans and Animals Get Sick Together* (Xuelin: Xuelin Press, 1989), and *Fantasy Poems and Drawings* (Shanghai: Fudan University Press, 1990).

The Moon Rises Slowly over the Ocean

It is time
We stand like children
On the silent beach
And calmly wait for the moon
Nothing has been lost on the moon today
A banana kazoo
Sucked between the lips of night
Is no longer blowing out of tune

Crisscrossed boughs set up an easel
The moon wearing a pure white suncap
Slowly comes over like a shy boy
Holding a transparent nylon net
With which to scavenge the ocean
Of its many broken hearts
Bobbing on the sea to the horizon

Young Poets (Qingnian Shiren), no. 7 (July 1983)

Purple Starfish

Majestic as it is, the great ocean
Lacks the strength to protect its children
A life is missing from those big breakers
It's no longer even a fresh piece of news
At a shop for sightseers I saw a small basket
Of starfish price-marked for sale

When milky jellyfish and medusas
Went with you to inspect the pure white coral reef
You were a proud little queen
With lilac-tinted light
     Shining over topshells and tiger cowries
Yet I spent only a couple of small coins to have you
Your soft body stiffened
As it lay on my palm

Only these five symmetrical antennae
Remained perked up
In self-confidence, yet in sorrow
As if you were telling me again and again
You had never hurt anyone
You longed for your little pals blowing blue bubbles
In the ocean during hide-and-seek games
At which dwarf sharks are forbidden to play

Man's world had seemed strange to you
Perhaps in the wreckage of a sunken ship
From a silken handkerchief embroidered
     With twin lotus blossoms and dandelion
You conjectured some human secret
One you must have begun to regret
When you were taken out of your paradise
    —The forest of pure snow coral

And I could not help regretting
That I made decorative patterns on my desk
Of your solidified tears
Now I have set up a miniature gravestone
In the quiet of my heart
If I had not known of your worldly existence
My heart would not have grown this heavy

Not all kindness
    Gets the respect it deserves
Not all injuries
    Are premeditated a long time
O starfish
Let's be friends
My heart will be your forest of coral

Shanghai Literature (Shanghai Wenxue), no. 4 (April 1983)

Late Wind

Under a brown branch I waited
Eagerly a long time for you
Yearned for you, Wind, who propel dandelions
To gently caress my sunburnt forehead
With your sleeve that flicks away frost flakes
To comb my frozen thoughts
With your fingers playing green
I would nuzzle snugly within your soft palm
And brandish my ruby ever so slightly—
A simple-minded, obstinate pursuit

I wanted you to pick me up
And stow me in a small purple basket
Let a troop comprised mostly of girls
Carry hope like shining dewdrops
Across dark mountains and rivers
Along tracks that cannot converge
But always advance shoulder to shoulder
Conveying to the north and the south
My definition of life with best wishes

It's a shame you are late, Wind,
For I got lost in the night's swaying

I smiled at a golden branch
That was reddened, tender and full
If a star had not reminded me
I wouldn't even have known I had gotten lost
In the sunshine with my own eyesight
I could see objects far, far away
I could see distant villages
With kitchen smoke singing soundless old songs

I longed to become a child's smile
And whisk an apple dream into a white pillow
The world won't sour into bitterness
Just because of me

I am the sun in children's eyes that can't scorch their hands
Around me life has sweets and moisture
Though I lost my flowers long ago
My heart is heavy with hidden fruit
Wind, even though you're late
I am already ripe

Shanghai Literature (Shanghai Wenxue), no. 4 (April 1983)

Yu Jian

(1954–) was born in Kunming in the southwestern province of Yunnan. On his father's side he is descended from landlords and on his mother's from coppersmiths. At age two, an antibiotic he was given for pneumonia caused severe hearing loss, and he says that as a result he was forced to create internal ears for himself. The Cultural Revolution, which began when he was twelve, brought about the closing of the school he attended. He was shocked to see many people in the street trampling over the names of national leaders in disgrace. He then became involved with gangs of thieves and homeless young people for a period of three years.

In 1969 he entered middle school, studied revolutionary theory, and then left to be a factory apprentice in a suburb of Kunming. From age sixteen to twenty-five, he worked as a lathe operator, welder, and farmer. Luckily, he found a well-stocked library that survived the Cultural Revolution, and he read there every Sunday for four years. The first American poem he read was Longfellow's "Song of Hiawatha." For half a year he submerged himself in the excitement of Whitman's *Leaves of Grass,* copying many of its lines into his notebook. Yu Jian had been writing regulated verse in imitation of Chinese classical poetry, then changed to free verse at age twenty. He says that he circulated his "Romantically flavored" poems among his friends, but could not publish them because magazines wanted sloganeering poems that eulogized revolution.

At age twenty-six, he began studying for his degree in Chinese literature at the University of Yunnan. His first poems were published in his sophomore year, and in 1984—the year of his graduation—he won the College Student Poetry Award from the magazine *Flying in the Sky (Feitian).* Later he was co-founder of an unauthorized poetry magazine in Nanjing called *They,* which exerted strong influence on the poetry of his contemporaries. Many of its contributing authors became important figures in a large group of poets known in the later 1980s as the "third generation."

Yu Jian has been working for the Theoretical Research Office of the Yunnan Literature and Art Federation. In 1989, his book

Sixty Poems was published by the Yunnan People's Press in Kunming. He summarizes his approach to writing as follows:

> My poetics contain no principles that can't be changed because creative writing has to be a process that continually develops and changes. The world is so rich and complex that we have to maintain sufficient enthusiasm and zest for all sorts of possibilities. Especially in a society like China's, which adopts "quiescence" as its philosophy of life, poets need an extra measure of creative vitality.
>
> Yet isn't there something a poet must adhere to steadfastly? I think this one thing is an absolute freedom in creating. To a certain extent, poets should keep an objective view of the world. The only thing they need to obey is the truth of poetry. And poets should not be manipulated or controlled by the social environment in which they find themselves.
>
> I prefer a plain, simple, and, at the same time, a rich and complex style in poetry. I especially admire the ability of great poets to insinuate the metaphysical by way of the most common and mundane things. One of my favorite poets, the American Robert Frost, has this ability. I'm opposed to deliberate obscurity in poetry. I especially oppose the allegorical tradition in classical Chinese poetry.
>
> Poetry is a tough occupation. Poets are craftsmen in a workshop rather than talents in a salon. Furthermore, I believe that poets as common people should work for the values that human beings commonly acknowledge—humanism, freedom, justice, and truth.

Opus 39

During the years crowds jammed the streets
You lit off by yourself for Xinjiang
Maybe it's not so bad out there in the boonies
You really looked outlandish in a crowd
Try on those jeans now and see
How well they've lasted
Only three and a half years' wear and still like new
Remember the time
You and I got into that heavy rapping
That made everybody around clam up
You never went in for banging my ears
How well you know in your heart
That we struggle all our lives
Just to put on a front of being human
Always at a loss for what to do
When we're around good looking women
We're too dumb to even know how dumb we are
One of those women looked me up once
Said what a shame   with your swell voice
You could have made it as a baritone
Sometimes I think of you borrowing my money
I would stand at my gate
Trying to spot you among the scruffy men
I know you're going to come back here some day
Three short novels and a bottle of booze in your arms

Sitting in that rattan chair from Sichuan
Speaking for a couple of hours
As if the whole world were your audience
Now and again you'll glimpse yourself in the mirror
Heart brimming with sudden rushes of joy
Afterward you'll watch me a while in dead silence
Then go home with the empty bottle under your arm

1983

High Mountains

A high mountain casts its shadow down upon the world
Making even the tallest man look puny
A person has to stay honest up in the mountains
He feels as if he's walking past heroes
He holds his tongue   afraid of losing strength
Honesty   a jet black rock
An eagle   a young tree with pointed leaves
You feel so much alive in high mountains
As you walk along their summits
Storms   floods and lightning
Are all perpetual forces up in the mountains
They bring ruin to mountains
Mountains ruin them too
They shape mountains
And mountains shape them
Mountain people are solitary
Only the flat ground is crammed with cooking smoke
You need a sailor's patience up in the mountains
The waves there never calm down   harbors never appear
As you lurch and sway
You find yourself rising to a crest
Or fallen back into a trough
Never in your life do you see a steady horizon
Climb a certain height   you can see a lot farther
But stand on one peak and you just see others
More and more of them and they keep getting higher

So you keep quiet   because you have to keep going
With no particular destination in mind
Many ordinary men and women in Yunnan
Have scaled many kingly mountains
And have finally been buried among those stones

1983

Rivers

In the high mountains of my homeland
Many rivers flowing through deep ravines
Hardly ever see the sky
No sails are hoisted aloft on those rivers
Nor does a boat song attract flocks of gulls
Only after scrambling across numberless mountain ridges
Can you hear the sound of those rivers
Perhaps aboard a raft of giant trees
You might dare float among their torrents
Some of this region will always remain unknown to people
Freedom in these parts belongs to eagles alone
River currents are brutal during the rainy season
Devastating winds from the plateau plunge huge boulders into
    valleys
And red mud dyes the rivers
As if blood flowed out of the great mountains
Only in tranquility
Can anyone see the plateau's swollen veins
People living on opposite banks of those rivers
Probably will never get a close look at one another's faces
Yet wherever you go in my homeland
You will hear people talking about these rivers
As if they were talking about their gods

1983

Modern Chinese Experimental Poetry

Wang Xiaolong

(1954–) was born on Hainan Island, a province in the South China Sea that produces coconuts, rubber, black tea, and coffee. According to a tradition in his family, when the Song Dynasty poet Su Shi was demoted and assigned to Hainan, he brought with him people of Han nationality, including someone named Wang, who may be the poet's forebear. Other family ancestors came from local ethnic minorities.

At the outbreak of World War II, Wang Xiaolong's father joined the Communist army on the mainland and became first-chair cellist and a conductor in a well-known revolutionary musical troupe. He led the troupe in company with the army to northeastern China, where he persuaded a young woman from a small, secluded town to flee her rigidly disciplined family for a life with him of revolution and art. She became the poet's mother.

In a personal statement, Wang Xiaolong explains his situation as a writer:

> My blood is a mixture of the tropical and frigid zones. The fierce conflict between the wildness of the south and the morality of the north fills my life with self-contradiction and unravelled nightmares. All the bad things, like trees on a boulevard, stand loyally along the streets I have walked as well as those I have yet to set foot upon.
>
> Beginning at seventeen, I worked eight years as a truck loader. Then I was involved in organizing large artistic activities for youth organizations in Shanghai, while in my spare time I lectured on modern poetry to middle school students. In 1980 I founded the Experimental Poetry Society and was principal editor of the anthology *Selected Experimental Poetry*.
>
> Youth and dreams have left me. I am now thirty-five years old with a six-year-old daughter and a family to take care of. I am currently working at a state-run video company where every day I confront low-grade movies from Hollywood. The only time I have for release is around midnight, when I keep smoking, keep reading, and keep writing poems that most people don't need.

Wang Xiaolong has published widely in Chinese magazines. The purview he communicates in poetry has been termed "non-emotionalization" *(wu qing hua)*. With philosophical underpinnings in Existentialism, he suggests that man has no privileged place in the universe and may be living a life no more meaningful than an insect's. The conclusion of his poem, "When We Finally Turn Fifty" alludes to a saying of Lao Zi: "Heaven and Earth are not benevolent, and treat all things as they treat a dog."

When We Finally Turn Fifty

We'll be just as we are now
Kissing as we casually fix a meal
Getting by whether or not the laundry's been done
No talking allowed during reading time
No money in the bank
Having a spat once every three days on average
Making our walk home from the movies
Deliberately long and sad
Then pretending we haven't known each other for three whole days
So we can be especially intimate on Sundays
The weather getting strangely pleasant
During the night we dream with our heads stuck together
And see two small dogs
Running across the snow

When we finally turn fifty

Selected Experimental Poetry (Tanfuo Shixuan)

Surgery Ward

Even the geranium in the hall is crestfallen
Those who walk in here inevitably hang their heads
They trundle off to bed after dinner
Staring with one hundred percent sympathy at a body
That seems to lack something under a snow-white bandage
Later on they deliberately turn up the radio to a loud wah-wah
As they imagine they're the great Maradona*
Or some fucking football kicked against the goalpost
Nobody comes this afternoon
That girl who brought one boy oranges and little smiles each
    afternoon
Won't be coming back anymore
Last night that boy
Took advantage of everyone's sleeping and stealthily died
This morning one old sparrow turned up to sob a while
Now it hides under who-knows-what eave pondering a line of poetry
Nobody comes this afternoon
The nurse sits like a man with one knee to her bosom
Writing a long letter that never comes to the last line
She flicks on the light and instantly the sky is black
After dark the mosquitoes' mouths loom especially large
This world—if it had no mosquitoes—this world
In spite of everything wouldn't be a bad place.

Source unknown

*Diego Armando Maradona is a famous Argentinean soccer player.

Irredeemable Mistakes

Strolling with your mistress you missed the fact that her eyes
Under that streetlight showed she had just lost the passion of her
 lover
Not until you tried locating the person did the address prove wrong
You forgot which bridge to cross while going home
Removed the ladder from under that bird's feet
And in winter cherished the memory of spring
Or discussed solitude with the President
You didn't lift your foot to shoot a goal
On the empty soccer field
You gave people photographs
Borrowed money from the rich
And wrote to people who would never write back
But the biggest mistake I remember ever making
Was to shop for a pair of shoes
For a friend who'd just had one leg sawn off

Poetry Magazine (Shikan), no. 3 (March 1987)

Beautiful Rain

Your long sleeves flap ever so lightly
Enveloping me and forcing me to walk behind you
So I do walk behind you
Flowing and swaying
We suddenly find ourselves at a crossroads
You point into the air with a willow twig
Mushrooms of umbrellas roil every which way on the street
Everyone appears to be in some kind of trance
Up and down the street people's drunken eyes look misty
I hear them talk incessantly in their dreams
You suggest that I get acquainted with everyone
So I set about getting to know them
Leaning against a wet billboard
I suddenly want to shout
Hey people yes you sophisticated people
The rooms you live in are too small
And everything is too expensive
You are too magnificent
Hey there people you sophisticated people
Why only on occasions like this
Do we get acquainted and smile at one another
While at other times
Out in the sun
We're all strangers everyone
So strange and serious

Poetry Magazine (Shikan), no. 3 (March 1987)

Yang Lian

(1955–) was born in Berne, Switzerland, returning to China with his parents during his first year. During the Cultural Revolution he settled in the country and he began writing poetry in 1976. Since the publication of his early poems in *Today (Jintian)*, the controversial and short-lived magazine of the obscurist poets, he has been identified with that group and has published articles in their defense. His poems also have appeared in major national magazines, and he has worked for the Central Broadcasting station in Beijing. During the early months of 1987 several of his books were banned. Yet he has continued to write poetry and has published a major work of criticism entitled *The Self-Awareness of Man*. In 1989 he visited Hong Kong and by mid-year emigrated with his wife and child to Auckland, New Zealand. The three recently moved to Australia.

Boy by the Sea
Preface to a New Collection of Poetry

I don't know who that boy is
The one playing an intriguing game by the sea
    Owner of a sand castle and daydreams
    A straw hat shading his eyes
    He's laughing robustly
    As he strolls together with the sun
I don't know who that boy is . . .

The handkerchief pinned to his shirt front
Is blue as the sky emblazoned with life's mysteries
    His face is a beautiful dream
    He whispers to himself
    He has come to the world's beach
    To talk to the waves
I don't know who that boy is . . .

I don't know whether his basket-like heart
Contains memories other than these
    The ocean overlaid with the rays of twilight
    Hiding laughter within an everlasting puzzle
    Even though storms hover past the horizon
    The world deserves the laughter of small children
I don't know who that boy is . . .

Poetry Magazine (Shikan), no. 5 (May 1982)

Plowing

I am a plow
I am a betrayer of cold and death
Endless fields come toward me
They carry spring's dreams
Coming toward me, the moistened moon—
My antique, exquisite body

I am grief
I hear the groans of roots being amputated
My heart is rolling and trembling
In black waves
Like a boat fighting the storm
Like a flag quietly hoisted in humiliation
I hand frozen clumps of deep earth to the sun
Making the tract claimed by loneliness and desolation
Yield a cheerful brook once again

I am serious love
I melt unlimited tenderness with an edge of steel
More sincere than an embrace and kisses
I force all wildness, poverty and hopelessness
Far away from the great land
I give my naked soul to love
Marching on forever, spreading eternal life—
Furrow upon furrow of trenches
Plot after plot of fields
Carry my longings that gradually stretch
And submerge into new green during a radiant season

Shanghai Literature (Shanghai Wenxue), no. 5 (May 1980)

Autumn

I

Night is a stagnant time
Time is the flow of night.
You stopped in the doorway
And briefly glanced back at me.

Is this goodbye?
Will everything between us be forgotten
As indifferent white snow covers everything
Once the glamorous autumn colors pass?

How I love and esteem fruit,
Yet I don't fear a tundra of refusal.
As long as the soul keeps drinking warm blood
No withering season looms in the future!

The autumn wind is swaying all those stars
—Ah, that's eternity writing in the sky;
Yes, one glance of yours is reason enough
For me to owe you my heart-felt thanks.

2

I thirst to be a bush whose leaves are dried,
Whose shadowy brown limbs time has compressed.
You would be the open countryside in early spring,
Letting me quietly melt in your warm sweet arms.

I long to be a wisp of straggling cloud,
Wrinkles of worry over my wan face.
You would be the delicate blue sky,
Wafting the last fond kiss at my funeral.

I long to be a sunken boat, a broken
Life sliding into the dark green abyss.
You would be pure holy spindrift, casting
Verses of mourning for me with all your soul.

I long to be a guidon of battle,
A dark purple spirit unfurling belief.
You would be the howling hot wind, offering
Annual sacrifice for my blood-drenched songs.

3

Wild geese thread to mist in the night sky,
Dour winter paces up and down the horizon.
The north wind, with insidious whistling,
Will soon bring cruel despair into the world.

Is this how autumn finally disappears—
Blanching all the color from my dreams?
Well, darling, what are you going to do?
Would you throw away my lonely sorrow?

Oh, you are not to blame any more
Than autumn can be master of her own fate.
The one goodbye tear I saw in your eye
Will make me love you deeply and forever.

I must go on and face the snowstorm,
Letting icy fire burn and explode my lungs.
With all its perseverance my soul asks:
Where are you, fresh new Green? When shall we meet?

JANUARY 1980

Stars (Xing Xing), no. 1 (January 1980)

The Mirror

If reality   could start from fantasy
Then glass would be our only scenery
The door opens   to the noise of a mercury waterfall
After the white daytime comes full circle
Another white daytime allied with dark night
Began from eyelashes   under the moon
Goose-egg shaped pebbles shed yellow light pale as a pawn ticket

In this room within a room
A noiseless auction is in session
Eyes exchange vicious desires with busts
Ants crawl over thin broken wrinkles near the corner of the mouth
Wild grass grows in all directions
Chased by the same deeply buried decomposing skeleton
Under both skin and clay   like snakes preparing for hibernation
The blood is a red-leaved woods rustling in the wind
And dies every time light shines upon it

In the swamp of glass   the fleet mercury bird
Stoops low   its face petrified
Time creates a labyrinth in which to lose itself

We are floating under the horizon
Both eyes bulging
Our four fishlike limbs entangle one another
As we pass below the bridge, the world hangs high overhead
Whoever peers into his own self
Will have to be born tragically

People's Literature (Renmin Wenxue), no. 3 (March 1988)

The Girl in Memory

After I breath deeply   then close my eyes
You come into my room
On a summer day   wild grass has the fingers of a song
Beneath your feet   memory is a quiet graveyard

No   please don't stoop to read the tombstone
Or mischievously search   for names just like your own
Don't mumble to them   or smile
That smiling voice which people might still remember
No no   that's just not you

Meadow I lay on at the age of nine
Sunbathing on green carpet woven completely of light
Rocks don't really understand all the things you love

Names spread in all directions   like a breeze
That starts with you   yet also dreams beyond your breath
And is forgotten not far away beneath the ground
Or even very far away   walks into the room that yearns for you
Even though you have never entered it

People's Literature (Renmin Wenxue), no. 3 (March 1988)

Scenery in a Room

I'm thirty-two years old   and have heard enough lies
No more of that scenery can be crammed into this room
A caller with a face like an ear of corn
Stands by the door hawking his moldering stones
His tongue showed   a kind of eternity ground between the teeth

They are all cold or you are   so cold that you
Want to be disgorged   like the obscene pictures on the wall
Memory is a queue of addresses dwindling to nothing
The autumn grass dies   beneath a bare foot of gold
Who leaned on the window and heard constellations disappearing
The sound of the wind at night   like a pear falling
After the empty room has been thrown out

Walking back and forth within your naked flesh
Limbs drop off   as if they were sky and water
The wet sun   wounded and yelling forgets everything
No more scenery can be moved into this scene

Until the last bird has fled into the sky
Collides with an open hand   and is frozen into a blue vein
This room is going to be ensconced in there
Whenever you lock yourself up   the echo of emptiness
Reciting the darkness
Is burying your heart's only scenery and its only lie

People's Literature (Renmin Wenxue), no. 3 (March 1988)

Betrayed

Around you   stand four vertical squares
Four shameless eyewhites that went crazy
A pregnant spider
Sighing   weaves a net for your ankles
You first turned back your head when dust shrouded your face
Yesterday you saw   that idea blackened
In a drop of blood from a bedbug
Nails grow pale   like a land of waterlogged saline-alkaline soil
Don't be scared   you said to the mirror
Both hands stop as if shocked as they touch mildewed patches
       that appear all over your body
Two chunks of gray-green ears press you from both sides
Don't be frightened   never has anyone betrayed himself
The mirror is also a square
Once you have sat in it   you feel comforted
From the dark part of your abdominal cavity
You've already been bleached   swollen   petrified
Into a thick white limestone mushroom

People's Literature (Renmin Wenxue), no. 3 (March 1988)

The Time and the Place

I can't go back to that old house
Any more than you can   even though
A lamp shines there all night   Hearing the tall dark shadow
Of the white poplar   outside the window
You're still expecting   some crescendo of eerie footsteps

Through all of autumn   only the wind has come to call
Turning over those red tiles one after another
The Lianchi flowers which in October look dismal as broken walls

Suddenly invade your dreams one night
And for the occasion   blossom elegantly all by themselves
At the old house which I know well but can't go back to visit
You cannot go back either   to old days that grow unfamiliar

The heart of music stopped beating without notice
The house hid in its own oblivion
Trees wrapped in green or sleep   once awakened
have already withered one leaf after another

The old days still reside   where our hands disappear
Names   removed   cautiously respect the same taboo
But when birds start singing every morning
Do you or don't you remember there's a darkness
Risen from silence   pouring out a more and more
Remote horizon   deep yellow undulating ridges on other planets
All roads have dissolved
This track becomes the only way to return

People's Literature (Renmin Wenxue), no. 3 (March 1988)

Ma Lihua

(1955–) lives in Lasha, Tibet, and is one of the
few writers in that country who enjoys a reputation throughout
China. Quite versatile, she has published collections of her poetry, as
well as fiction and reportage. Her work shows influences of Taoism,
Buddhism, and Western modernism. The following selection of four
poems constitutes a sequence entitled "My Sun."

Waiting for Sunrise

Let the eyes traverse the mountain
To meet the sunrise

He has framed the eastern pasture
In scarlet lace
Will the eternal lamp
That I share with the universe
    Come striding out on his vermilion carpet

For a long while   I stand on the grassy lowland
Knowing he is still too far away
Yet I believe it is possible to reach his brilliance and warmth
That is enough.   I allow
    My heart to feel exaltation or calm
    And my love for him to ascend and deepen

Let the eyes traverse the mountain
To meet the sunrise of the living

Injured hearts become more and more frail
So fragile they cannot continue resisting the temptation of
    disillusionment
When the small boat was led to an undertow in the cold spring
The strong sun's wind blew open the sail of destiny one more time
It is truly worthwhile to have one last overreaching desire
To sail toward that remote shore of gold
Sun O Sun
Let's not be on guard against each other

The sun has risen to a half circle
Like an eye or a brow on a smiling face
I belong to him and want to snuggle my back against him
Open both my arms high in an arc
Then take a gigantic picture against the light
Yes, there's the pasture—the sun—
 And my own dark silhouette

Collected Poetry of Exploration

The Sun Is Out

He comes sounding twelve thousand wind chimes
Saturating the universe with harmonious echoes of majesty
Flooding the watery pasture on which everything is visible at a
    glance
The sun raises vast tides

Sunlight combs my torrential thoughts
Extending them into a thick mane of cirrus
That moves parallel to the sun's track
In a wilderness where clumps of grass predominate
It's best to be a tall, straight sunflower.

Or could someone transform me into a cloud
So I could approach him on wings borrowed from the solicitous wind
I'd also be content as a rocky cliff standing erect since the world
    began
Eroded by wind into flying dust that settles back onto the great earth
Accepting the ceaseless caress of the sun
Or else could someone make me coextensive with Eros

Blades of grass flicker like swaying Buddhist streamers
Praying not for fortune but for love
The lives under the sun simply recite a magic word
I say secretly, Do you know
The creator made me for you alone
And designed me for your sake
Only I am able to decode
    The riddle of our destined relationship
I choose the pen of poetry only for the sun
Yes only for you the sun

The surging grassland suddenly becomes serene
Feeling a much deeper fresh state of turbulence
A host of sculls rises in seriousness and beauty
Their eyes all saluting in the same direction
Distant hymns pulsate faintly in chords
Where and from what century does that sound begin

Collected Poetry of Exploration

Midday

penetrates me with brilliance and fills me to the brim
Heart purified to crystaline clarity
No trace of clouds in the sky
And hence no shadow beside me
The sun and I
Coincide vertically in the brightest of angles

Stay motionless in any relaxed posture
And for as long as you do not open your eyes
You melt into one being with the sunlight

The sun turns the heart's agitation into tranquility
And love becomes profound because of it, after sublimation.

Collected Poetry of Exploration

The Sun at Dusk

Separated by huge expanses of time and space
I gaze ahead
Sight communicates in the language of the universe
I should probably laugh, sing a farewell song
And ask a gray swan to be my messenger, to carry the song in its
    beak
And to merge goldenly with the light at dusk
This may be the time for me to actualize my overreaching fantasies
Sail that small boat to the shore of gold
Experience the daily tides of love
Emotions transformed into a bountiful ocean

Beauty of tragic heroism
And tranquility
Farewell, my sun
A handkerchief of color-laden clouds waves at the setting sun
A treasury of good wishes to you all the way home
A treasury of good wishes

A pastoral tune sung at evening
I sigh for the silence in my heart
And so my mind closes a window and walks into our nightlong
    mutual yearning

Whoever indulges in fantasy and tires of waiting
Will inevitably misspend
The night and merely wait in silence, but the night
No longer chants about moonlight, and never chants
About that sliver of lunar ice so easily burst asunder
My sun is the one that never makes a promise
My sun is the one that never breaks an appointment

Collected Poetry of Exploration

Liang Xiaobin

(1955–) was born in Shandong Province. During the Cultural Revolution he worked as a peasant in the countryside. He has also been a factory worker. In 1979 he began publishing his poetry.

China, I Lost My Key

China, I lost my key.
More than ten years ago,
I ran distracted down the red street
Till I came to deserted fields in the suburbs.
I screamed violently and then
I lost my key.

Ah soul, my wretched soul
Was unwilling to wander anymore.
I wanted to go home,
Rummage through drawers for childhood pictures,
And look at green trillium leaves
Pressed between book pages.

What's more—
I also wanted to open the bookcase
And take out my volume of Heine's *Selected Poems*
On a date that I had planned.
I would show this book to my girlfriend
As a sign of my love
Shot like a flare into the sky.

All this,
This whole beautiful stratagem couldn't come true.
China, I lost my key.

Rain poured from the sky again.
My dear key,
Where are you lying?
I've wondered whether wind and rain have corroded you
Or you might be stained with rust.
No, I don't think so;
I'll try persistently to search for you
And hope to find you again.

And you, great sun,
Have you seen my key at all?
I hope your brilliant light
Shines ardently upon it.

I walk the vast fields
Tracing the footprints of my soul.
All that I have lost
Is under my careful scrutiny.

DECEMBER 1979–AUGUST 1980

Poetry Magazine (Shikan), no. 10 (October 1980)

The Snow-White Wall

Mother,
I saw a snow-white wall.

This morning I went up the street to buy crayons
And I saw a workman
Striving with all his might
To whitewash a long enclosure wall.

He looked and smiled over his shoulder at me,
And he asked me to tell all the children:
    Don't scribble a mess on the wall anymore.

Mother,
I saw a snow-white wall.

That wall used to be filthy,
Scrawled with many violent, brutal words.
Mother, you once wept
Over those very curses.

Daddy is gone,
Gone forever.

The wall that's so white,
Whiter than the milk I drink,
Has been flashing through my dreams.
It stands on the horizon
Shimmering with enchanting light in the daytime.
I love pure white.

I'll never draw a mess on the wall,
Never will.
Blue sky, gentle as my Mother—
Did you hear me?

Mother,
I saw a snow-white wall.

MAY–AUGUST 1980

Poetry Magazine (Shikan), no. 10 (October 1980)

The Story of a Bolt

With a cold steel wrench
I removed a rusty bolt
Which now lies in the big hand
Of my boss, the master mechanic.

I had a lot of trouble
Avoiding his curious stare.
The bolt,
Like my heart,
Bounced a bit in fear
On the master mechanic's palm.

I admit
It got rusty from corrosion.
A bolt could have a random thought or two,
It hasn't been able
To keep its shine so well.

Now the bolt is waiting for a verdict
As the master mechanic looks on.
Over there is a scrap barrel—
Will I be thrown away, or cleaned up
And screwed back into where I was before?

Stars (Xing Xing), no. 8 (August 1982)

Real Kissing

A real kiss isn't so wonderful as one in legend
A real one is hardly more than coarse soap touching soft soap

Three P.M. was the time she set aside for kissing
We embraced, I a big tumor inside her body
She went to work after excising the tumor
     and covering it with a blanket

My only shortcoming was absentmindedness while we kissed
She discovered my wrist twisting in darkness behind her
"Just like a man! Checking your watch even while you kiss."

A real kiss isn't so savory as an imagined one
Once myths pile up, the intimate kiss fades away

Poetry Magazine (Shikan), no. 8 (August 1986)

Wang Xiaoni

(1955–) was born in north China and at age thirteen settled in the countryside with her parents. In 1978 she began studies in the Chinese Department at Jilin University and, after graduation, worked as an editor for a prestigious film studio. She is a member of the Chinese Writers' Association of Jilin.

She married the poet and critic Xu Jingya, and they have one child. In 1982 her husband wrote and published a controversial defense of obscurist poetry, was arrested for it by police in Changchun (capital of Jilin Province), and then was forced to recant his views through self-criticism. After rehabilitation he became literary editor of the *Shenzhen Youth Daily,* but was sacked because of a serious ideological difference in 1987. Both Wang and Xu have been unemployed since then and are living in Guangdong Province. Although local authorities have told them to return to their place of origin in Jilin, they also say that they would not be given work even if they did go back. The two have chosen not to return, perhaps because they were also persecuted in Jilin.

Going Astray

Back lane, eons long and dark blue, that I should have known long
   ago.
Back lane across ice and snow, without sound or a lasting footprint.
   As I entered it
   sun and moon hung
   in mid-sky at one time.
   Ahead or behind
   the deep lane
   recedes.

I firmly believe no idea could penetrate its two rose-colored walls.
The warm air I exhale falls straight into icicles adorning the ground.
   Friends,
   I heard
   many voices
   familiar as my own.
   I know
   you are all
   close and also
   far away.

Someone up in the air is calling me loudly again and again.
With bowed head I must avoid every eye that might stir my heart.
   Many things could
   keep me very busy
   for my whole life.
   The most important
   is to traverse
   this narrow trail
   silently and alone.

Three Hundred Lyric Poems by Modern Young Poets

Dark Night on a Southbound Train

On this night
dark as pitch
countless black wheels
pump through
invisible space.

I stretch
out all
my fingers
yet can't feel
any familiar breath.
Without that pair of hands
even a burning match
seems quite dark.
Nothing here
but my all-black valise
and the long
night.

Closing my eyes
I salute
the blue door
with my imagination.
A greeting from anyone
kind enough to penetrate
this dark night
would make the mountains, rivers
and roads all glisten.

The Wind is Roaring

The wind roared through the sky above my head.
Louder and softer by turns,
it was laden half with grief
and half with bad luck.
An old man
walked with difficulty by my side
holding his thick cotton cap to his head
as the wind kept on roaring.

The wind roared in the chambers of my ears.
Stronger and weaker by turns,
it was laden half with dignity
half with exuberance.
A boy
ran cheerfully beside me,
his hand full of bits of colored paper
that he let go of all at once
as the wind kept roaring.

Suddenly I couldn't help feeling happy—
my black hair
flying and singing in the wind.

Poetry Magazine (Shikan), no. 8 (August 1980)

Li Qi

(1956–) was born in north China and began writing poetry at age fourteen. She is now a college teacher. Her poems have appeared in many national and provincial magazines.

Spring Night

On this calm, quiet spring night
The moon gleams in the sky
Lamp shadows lace the ground

Pairs of lovers whisper under trees
Couples stroll along the river.
But ten thousand mountains separate you and me—
I, on a quiet campus
You, in a faraway barracks . . .

We've always been ordinary persons
Like the two smallest stars
On the horizon . . .
Yet we also have the pride of common people
Who willingly offer up our rendezvous
For the sake of our motherland

The evening breeze is gentle and slow,
The moonbeams harmonious and warm,
My eager gaze and yours
Intersect at the North Star.

Women's Lyric Poetry

Ice Carvings

Ice carvings look strikingly
Beautiful because a warm heart
Molded them
In harsh northern cold.

It seems I came to know this
Through the caress and courage
Of harsh winter. Soft water
Can stand up robustly too
And show life's miracle
Through a variety of postures.

These melt when spring comes,
Melt without a sigh
After having stood so proudly.
Happily they come into being;
Happily they accept departure.

Let the North
Carve me likewise—
Carve me into a lively fawn
Into a cheerful fish
Into a peacock or a swallow.
Even though I disappear
One day, I disappear
Into springtime's smile.

Three Hundred Lyric Poems by Modern Young Poets

Grandfather

Snowflakes are dancing in the air
And suddenly I believe I see my old grandfather.
His figure seems so clear,
Yet at the same time so blurred.

While he lived he was just an ordinary person
Whose back was bent
Like an old tree with all its leaves fallen.
When it snowed he would go outside
Quietly to clear the walk
And then—something like the way I scan poetry—
He would study footprints backwards and forwards
In the road.

Now that he has passed away
He lies in the vast, deep earth.
While the snowflakes fly,
Does his soul perhaps
Still remember that sacred duty?
Oh, I will go out
Following in his steps
To clear the walkway.

Women's Lyric Poetry

Gu Cheng

(1956–) was born in Beijing, the son of the poet Gu Gong, who was a cultural worker with the communist army before the liberation of 1949. The entire family was exiled in 1969 to Chang Bei County in Shandong Province, where Gu Cheng worked for four years as a swineherd while studying writing and painting. In 1974 he was reassigned to carpentry in a Beijing street repair station. In 1979 he published his first poems in *Today* and participated in its literary activities. The following year his work unit was disbanded. By 1983 he had published three hundred pieces, but the Beijing Writers' Association still refused to assign him a job. In the space marked "Occupation" on his membership card, he wrote the standard phrase for unemployment: "Waiting for work." One of the best known obscurist poets, he published *Selected Lyrics of Shu Ting and Gu Cheng* in Fujian in 1982, and *Selected Poems by Bei Dao and Gu Cheng* was published by Good Book Press in Sweden in 1983. A poetry collection entitled *Dark Eyes* was published by People's Literary Press in Beijing in 1986, and *Collected Poems of Gu Cheng* was published by New Horizon Press in 1987. A French translation of his poems, entitled *Les Yeux Noirs,* was published in Paris by Les Cahiers Confluent in 1987, and an English translation, *Selected Poems of Gu Cheng,* was published by Renditions Press in Hong Kong in 1990. A Danish translation, published in 1989, is entitled *Gu Cheng Sorte ojne.* He is a member of the Chinese Writers' Association. Since 1988 he has lived with his wife and child in Auckland, New Zealand, where he teaches at the university.

Early Spring

Morose, the sky hangs back:
Will there be snowflakes? or raindrops?

A muddy river flows fast:
Is it pursuing? or escaping?

Far from here lovers part:
A prologue? or epilogue?

October (Shiyue), no. 1 (January 1981)

Scenery

A distant river turns purple,
The waves suddenly begin to rush away.

A storm hoists a black flag,
A net of rain drags across the earth.

Reefs wilfully cast off bubbles
As if they were only pennies.

Small craft poke up their masts
Like arms stretched in one last prayer.

The sun has still not returned
But smiles deceptively now and again.

October (Shiyue), no. 1 (January 1981)

One Generation

Dark night endowed me with eyes for darkness*
Yet with them I seek light

Stars (Xing Xing), no. 3 (March 1980)

*During the Cultural Revolution, Chinese writers were told not to write about the "darkness" of life in their society. This dark side was supposed to include personal feelings of melancholy, an emotion that, if expressed, could dampen the public morale.

Precipices

Two huge stone escarpments are closing tightly
Leaning toward each other bit by bit.

What searing animosity it must be
That scorches and bends their iron-dark bodies.

Tree-root tendons strain taut;
Rocky muscles stretch to full height.

When just one more dewdrop has fallen,
Ferocious wrestling will break out.

Yet this droplet suddenly crystalizes
Under pressure as time itself solidifies.

So this ancient hatred, still well preserved,
Stirs a little tremor of surprise in me today.

Stars (Xing Xing), no. 3 (March 1980)

Spring Scenery

The thawing riverbank
Ferments beneath the sun,
The pendulous willow leans into the breeze;
Beside her a tall poplar
Wears his heart upon his sleeve.

Long willow switches touch the water,
Splashing ring after ring of bright silver ripples;
A startled fish dives deep,
Bearing a scar from an old hook.

Stars (Xing Xing), no. 3 (March 1980)

Parting

In spring,
You delicately waved your handkerchief.
Were you telling me to go far away?
Or to come back at once?

No, it doesn't mean anything
And doesn't amount to anything.
It's like a flower fallen into the river,
Like a pearl of dew resting on the flower.

Only the shadows comprehend,
Only the wind perceives,
Only the richly colored butterfly startled by a sigh
Keeps flying back over the heart of the flower . . .

Stars (Xing Xing), no. 3 (March 1980)

Far and Close

You
Look a while at me,
Look a while at a cloud.

I feel
You are far away while looking at me,
So very close while looking at the cloud.

Poetry Magazine (Shikan), no. 10 (October 1980)

The Flag

Death is just a minor operation
That simply cuts out life
Without even leaving a scar

After surgery the patient lies in an eerie calm
Like an island sleeping in a bed
The thunderstorm hasn't quite passed
And around the white harbor entry
A fleet of whaling ships gathers

For the sake of living on and on
People have invented souls
Have invented free and unhampered sails
That do not suffer the torture of ropes
And can sail on dry land

The Contemporary Age (Dang Dai), no. 4 (April 1980)

Reunion by Design

Wheels completely stained with coaldust
Rattle down the middle of the road
We meet again

They say that I'm already old
Have forgotten how to leap
And have a smile just like a broken rice-stalk
But you—how shall I say—
Have eyes like drops of golden honey
Are healthy enough to still want to rule the world
And shine like the morning sun on fresh bread

The signal at the railroad crossing raises his arm
While the long-horned beetle drops its antennae

You ask me
What I'm doing nowadays
I say that I'm writing a fable
On the edges of a plaza
There are many steps
Very uneven, like worn-out teeth
Their rifts fill up with sand and dust
It's my duty to take a stroll over there
And study the traffic rules
Of ants that climb up along a cross

Naturally jobs like this
Are very few and far between

The sky is almost black
Go with your back turned
Let the red and green marketplace sing behind you
The flowers are about to wilt
Still surrounded by green foliage
Big warm cows are smiling on one side
As they shoot their pure white milk into the night

Once the heart is at rest
The blood still has to flow for many more years

The Contemporary Age (Dang Dai), no. 4 (April 1980)

Shell of Pearl

The pearl oyster shell was thrown down
On the sandy rock,
Stepped upon and broken,
Its pained yet expensive heart
Was then dug out,
Strung together
With countless other hearts and pains.

Its childhood dream extinguished
Its hallucinatory neon
Obscured by craze marks,
Its soft flesh
Left melting in the tide,
Although its sharp point of hatred
Was not yet ground blunt.

Perhaps at some future dawn,
The sun's brightening shape
Will threaten life once again.
The greedy pearl fisherman
Will again renew his quest.
The pearl oyster shell will then become
A miniature dagger,
And dirty blood mingled with the rosy light of dawn
Will smear its blade.

The Contemporary Age (Dang Dai), no. 4 (April 1980)

Farewell

Today
You and I
Are stepping over that venerable threshold
Don't offer blessings
Don't say goodbye
To do so would sound like a performance
Better to keep silence
Concealing isn't necessarily deceptive
Why not leave memories for the future
Just as we leave dreams in the night
Or tears in the sea
And wind in the sails

Wenhui Monthly (Wenhui Yuekan), no. 6 (June 1981)

Tang Yaping

(1962-) is a native of Sichuan who graduated with a degree in philosophy from Sichuan University. He is a poet of what is called the fifth generation and has been working as an editor at a television station in Guizhou Province.

Black Marsh
From *Black Desert*

Dusk is a dim and hazy time
So indistinguishable it must cause even dogs to doubt
I was always suspicious and I always fidgeted
I let down my long hair which flowed like dark night's wish to
    conquer
My desire was absolute blackness
I touched the blackest place for a long time
Watching it become a black whirlpool
That could entice the sun and moon with its force
So terror emerged and like night found no escape
My secret that night was utterly exposed in panic
My only courage was born in dejection
The last of my guts were born in death
So either give up everything or hold onto everything
I walk resolutely into the black marsh
I was born suspicious but credulous as well
I caused my mother cramps before my birth
Tonight evil dreams will penetrate thin ice
Entrap and submerge my memories
I have flooded everything I wanted to
Only one bundle of age-old sunlight remains unconquered
My silence has clogged the throat of black night

Modern Chinese Experimental Poetry

Black Nightgown

I poured water for foot washing
Into a bottle too deep to fathom
A rainy night has the most savory of implications
I invited a man over to shoot the breeze
With no idea before he came of how it would turn out
I closed the purple drapes and lit the ruddy wall lamp
The black nightgown swayed in a circle in my room
There were three raps at the door
He stepped in with a black umbrella
And stood in the middle of the floor
We began by drinking strong tea
Sublime flattery flows like running water
Sweet lies are soul-stirring as the stars
I leaned back casually on the sofa
And with scholarly detachment told the fable of a spinster
Then the god started to flee from our midst
Stopping up her ears and leaving one slipper behind
Nighttime boasting has a blurring effect
Whenever a story's to be told
The darker it gets the better
The harder it rains the better

Modern Chinese Experimental Poetry

One Hundred Roses

One hundred spring mornings weep for me
They become one hundred autumn twilights
The sword is the longest of paths
One hundred roses bring no comfort to the tomb
One hundred winters I will sleep in your arms
I am a child who has run himself ragged
Only you can embrace all my dreams
And calm me to the rhythm of my own heartbeat

Sleeping soundly in your arms I am transformed into a hundred
    infants
I curl to your breast and suck in your body's heat
I am a child crying bitterly with fatigue
Only your kiss can sip my tears
Can give me peace as deep as an ancient well

In your arms I'll sleep soundly for one hundred winters
I'll divide into one hundred nude young women and one hundred
    roses
I'll brew a choking liquor and hot blood
I am a child tired out from loneliness and growth
Only your crazy rhythm gives birth to my confidence and pride
I accept the comfort of strength

Poetry Magazine (Shikan), no. 1 (January 1987)

He Xiaozhu

(1964–) is a high school graduate who makes his living by touring the countryside with a government-sponsored music and drama group that presents entertainments not unlike vaudeville in the West. He is among the most accomplished of a group of Sichuan writers who refer to themselves as the fifth generation of poets writing since the end of the Cultural Revolution. They call their group "Fei Fei"—which means "No No." Less political than their predecessors, they use dreamlike imagery that somewhat recalls European surrealism. Because their avant-gardist posture of obscurantism disturbs the editors of established literary magazines, self-publication is the only way these poets' work could find an audience in the People's Republic of China. The four poems included here appeared in the magazine *Fei Fei: Poetical Works and Poetics*, published privately in Chengdu by this group.

Ann Saw a Red Rooster at a Funeral

Once the snow has perched upon a branch
You think the white sheet larger than you imagined
From now on you keep rehearsing
The white side in your black-and-white dreams
But real snow and that branch are already very far away

You're struggling to recall
Each match as it struck a light
But the huge white cloth left no warm ash
A man's beard is as cold as mice in snow
You don't remember the black side
Of what has impelled you so far

I'm still extending my open hands
You narrate the funeral from lines in my palm
Yet the worlds we dream won't reappear
Amnesia lies heaped in the forehead
Later you speak of two red mushrooms
The wilderness like a white cloth hides them away
And wraps my hands where memory reemerges

Ann, there is nobody in this room
Just me smoking a cigar

Fei Fei: Poetical Works and Poetics, no. 1 (1986)

Human Heads and Birds

I can't find a language
To convey the experience
Human beings right from the beginning
Have disguised themselves as birds
Up till now I still cannot reveal to you
That eyebrow that's been wretched for a long time

Each time you look at me
Your face lacks expression
Just like the time you saw
That picture of my family genealogy
The key figure in that picture is a star
Still showing grandma's fingerprint
Up till now I still haven't found
A language to explain it to you

In August
We made an excursion
Those mountains were really very easy
But try as we might we couldn't find our way out
Every picture carved in rock lacked
The eyes that you were looking for.
Human beings right from the beginning
Have disguised themselves as birds
The only thing I have that can account for this
Is my own two lips that still keep silence

MARCH 22, 1986

Fei Fei: Poetical Works and Poetics, no. 1 (1986)

Ann's Dream of Apples and Fish

I still haven't said
That deadly mushrooms must surely grow inside a large house
It's your endless dreaming of apples and fish
In a big house like this one
That scares me most

You have never gone behind the house
Into that black forest that I wrote about
You're constantly reaffirming the world you dream
Constantly saying
How much it's like the real world

We won't live here very long
I'll put a lock on every door
And lock shut the fishes' mouths with grass stalks
All the way up till dawn
Do you still expect to wrap your head
With a blanket during the rainy season
While you listen to those crackling sounds
Of a vast house rotting?

Fei Fei: Poetical Works and Poetics, no. 1 (1986)

A Language

I prefer not to
Speak that kind of language
At two in the afternoon

These two things are
The sleepy eyes of an owl
Who was struck dead by a phantasm
A presentiment of a snowy mountain death

Look where I'm pointing
And walk in that direction
Walk straight ahead
And then you'll hear the voice of a bell

I prefer not to
Speak that kind of language
Before the sky turns black

For a time we all sat
In front of a door
Waiting for sunset
Quietly telling our black beads

If a person has walked
Through the wasteland I seem to have walked through
And then walks toward the world
I still have nothing to say
I simply join my palms
This my last admonition

Fei Fei: Poetical Works and Poetics, no. 1 (1986)

Selected Chinese Texts

梦

艾青

醒着的时候
只能幻想
而梦
却在睡着的时候来访

或许是童年的青梅竹马
或许是有朋友来自远方

钢丝床上有痛苦
稻草堆上有欢晤

匮乏时的赠予
富足时的失窃

不是一场虚惊
就是若有所失

1980年春

酒

艾青

她是可爱的
具有火的性格
水的外形

她是欢乐的精灵
哪儿有喜庆
就有她光临

她真是会逗
能让你说真话
掏出你的心

她会使你
忘掉痛苦
喜气盈盈

喝吧，为了胜利
喝吧，为了友谊
喝吧，为了爱情

你可要当心
在你高兴的时候
她会偷走你的理性

不要以为她是水
能扑灭你的烦忧
她是倒在火上的油

会使聪明的更聪明
会使愚蠢的更愚蠢

距 离

蔡其矫

在现实和梦想之间
你是红叶焚烧的山峦
是黄昏中交集的悲欢；
你是树影，是晚风
是归来路上的黑暗。

在现实和梦想之间
你是信守约言的鸿雁
是路上不预期的遇见；
你是欢笑，是光亮
是烟花怒放的夜晚。

在现实和梦想之间
你是晶莹皎洁的雕像
是幸福照临的深沉睡眠；
你是芬芳，是花朵
是慷慨无私的大自然。

在现实和梦想之间
你是来去无踪的怨嗔
是阴雨天气的苦苦思念；
你是冷月，是远星
是神秘莫测的深渊。

（选自《诗刊》1981年7期）

祈　求

蔡其矫

我祈求炎夏有风，冬日少雨，
我祈求花开有红有紫；
我祈求爱情不受讥笑，
跌倒有人扶持；
我祈求同情心——
当人悲伤
至少给予安慰
而不是冷眼竖眉；
我祈求知识有如泉源
每一天都涌流不息，
而不是这也禁止，那也禁止；
我祈求歌声发自各人胸中
没有谁要制造模式
为所有的音调规定高低；
我祈求
总有一天，再没有人
象我作这样的祈求！

一九七五年
（原载《作品》1979年第1期）

珍　珠

郑敏

在海底沉睡，多少年？
光阴不是白白逝去，
虹彩在凹凸的珠面
自由地闪光，泛出微红。
真的珍珠
不是最完美的珍珠。

那按时培植的珍珠，
饱满而圆润的珠面，
一把，一样大小，
在美丽的腕、胸、颈上
炫耀光华，最完美的珍珠，
但……不是真的珍珠。

还有什么比美德更象珍珠，
那最真的也许不是看来最美的，
那看来最美的也许不是最真的，
我的心灵总是被
那凹凸不平的珠面吸引着
因为它有大海的消息，
它有令人神往的真挚。

（原载《长江》1982年第1期）

大都会素描

雁翼

一
一千万人共有多少轮胎？
在大马路上寻觅着，
我们时代的要求——快！

二
而每一个十字路口的上空，
红灯和绿灯，同志的语言，
叙述着沉重的爱。

三
多么矛盾的景象呵，
一个热恋着快速，
一个热恋着停滞。

四
没有绝对的胜利，
也没有绝对的失败——
维护着运转的世界。

五
我不敢歌颂绿，
我怕速度发疯发狂，
把我整个的爱毁坏！

六
我也不敢歌颂红——
它可能很安全，
但安全也许是一种人生的癌。

七

复杂而又简单的学问，
把多少政治家和科学家，
头发眉毛都愁白。

八

也许，世界生活是中性的，
用快批判着慢，
同时，用慢批判着快。

(选自雁翼诗集《雪迎征鸿》)

锯的哲学

流沙河

是的。锯片在锯木，
可是木也在锯锯片。
所以锯片也会钝，
而且愈锉愈窄，
总有一天会断。

木被锯成板了，
做成家具了。
锯片断了，
被抛弃了。

1972年

我的乐观主义

邵燕祥

我是一成年人
我的乐观主义也是成年的乐观主义

我的乐观主义
不是总在那里微笑的
它在泥泞里滚过
它在铁砧上经受过锤击
它在锤击下喷出火花
它在几乎熄灭的篝火里燃烧
人们曾轻蔑地叫它死灰

它受过棒打
受过揉搓
然后在冰冷刺骨的河水里漂过
它的每一根纤维
都一尘不染了
它不是一件工作服
它是我的乐观主义

我的乐观主义
不是一件衣服
有时穿上，有时脱去
更不是揣在衣服口袋里的良心
有时候随身携带
有时候丢在家里

我的乐观主义
是当它遭到践踏的时候
当许多它拥抱过的人也抛开了它的时候
投入我的怀里
我用我的体温把它煜热的

我煨热了它
它也煨热了我

它被出卖过
它被告过密
它一步一跌地长大了
没有经历过挫折的
没有见识过卑鄙的
不是成年的乐观主义

已经成年的乐观主义
并不总是甜蜜的
有时它甚至满面泪痕
我听到它吞声饮泣
但总是它，先从悲戚失望中醒来
拉住我的手
抚着我的心
捧起我的头
用只有大人对孩子那样的口吻
轻声细语地给我以慰藉
我的乐观主义长大了
它倒以为我会象小孩子似的灰心丧气
唉，我这个形影相随的老朋友
我的饱经忧患的乐观主义

(选自《上海文学》1984年第5期)

等　待

邵燕祥

不是四月那个新晴的上午
也不是那一带整齐的枫树林
没有阳光和雨滴
同时从五角的嫩叶上
滑进我的衣领

已经是十一月的夜晚
连我的心中
也下着凄凉的秋雨
秋雨透过破伞似的
疏疏落落的法国梧桐
落在我的破伞上
比行人的脚步更急

匆匆的行人稀少了
我站在迷离的街灯影里
我站在快要落尽叶子的梧桐树下
我站在被风吹斜的深秋的夜雨中
等你

不再是四月那个上午
初夏的绿色的枫树林
等待你的却还是
那曾经徒然等待你的人

我在十一月的深夜
在梧桐树下等你
秋雨单调而絮叨地
打着我的破伞
又打着我焦灼的心

天上的雨下得紧了
我心中的雨下得更紧
秋夜的梧桐雨真是凄凉
而我心中的雨是温热的
不用强迫，我的心
相信：初夏的上午你虽失约
深秋的雨夜你必定会来临

1980年10月1日

崇　拜

雷抒燕

山：
　我是人类塑像的基座。

太阳：
　从右手抛出，落进左手，
　我是他手中的金苹果。

水：
　看见纯洁的心，
　我才感到自己的混浊。

猩猩：
　人的美，
　使我羞于走出山林。

星：
　用千百只眼睛注视地球，
　我是羡慕人。

上帝：
　集中了一切美，
　我依然比人逊色。

时间：
　有了人，
　我才结束了昏睡。

天空：
　我的无穷变幻，
　是模仿着人的喜怒哀乐。

未来：
　　有了人，
　　才有了我。

大理石：
　　人，
　　给了我美和生命。

沙漠：
　　我的悲哀和丑陋，
　　在于藐视人类。

宇宙：
　　一切暗淡在我怀里的星，
　　都在人类手中放出光明。

美：
　　我骄傲，
　　我是人的影子。

没有仇恨，
没有性的冲动，
也没有激烈的辩论……

啊，聪明的科学家，
造出如些完美的"人"，
一切为人也无法克服的缺点，
都被它淘汰殆尽。

没有疾病，
没有愿望，
没有多余的话，
也没有怀疑和失信……

没有悲哀，
没有创造，
生存，仅仅是
为一道指令而生存。

我深深地悲哀，
为人的复制品
——假人！

1980年8月，北京
（原载《海韵》1981年第3集）

悬崖上的红杜鹃

徐刚

你悬崖上的红杜鹃，
对着我莞尔一笑，
却使我心惊胆颤！
在峡谷里粉身碎骨——
美，从来都是面临着灾难。

你悬崖上的红杜鹃，
在山风中却把枝叶梳理，
才使我悄悄心宽。
是的，你不是故作艰险，
也不是随遇而安，
你只是告诉我：美，就是自然！

谁想去采摘吗？
送给恋人
或者挂在自己的胸前；
悬崖上没有路，
有路的地方没有杜鹃，
倘若有谁真的走到它身边，
他的心上定会开一朵杜鹃……

你悬崖上的红杜鹃，
真象是黄山的笑容：
甜蜜中带着狡猾，
亲近中带着疏远，
你会使每一个人想起自己的初恋，
哦，那已经过去的岁月，
有时，真象悬崖上的红杜鹃……

1982年5月写于黄山 改于杭州

烟头

徐刚

我的烟头是我的森林，
我是个虔诚的"吸毒者"，
没有烟，太孤单，
我爱火，爱光明。
没有太阳的阴天，
我的火也不会熄灭，
想象的翅膀一样升腾。
谁也离不开被埋葬的一天，
我愿埋葬在我自己的森林……

纤　绳

叶延滨

1

我的命运
一段短短的历程
从肩到船

从一颗拳头大的年轻的心房
那收缩的肌腱
我传递着一个生命
给沉重而苍老的船

在船获得生命的瞬间
我也获得生命
—— 从渗血的肩

2

我有过童年——
绿色的幻想
太阳父亲般的抚爱

当我筋强力壮的时候
我离开了温馨的土地

一位头发苍白的母亲
用龟裂的手
把我搓揉

她的儿子又要溯流拉船
我是她扯不断的恋眷

3

把弯曲的河床拉直
使笔直的脊梁弯曲
——我是低沉的船夫曲
那铅一般沉重的旋律

绝壁上为我筑起栈道
运河堤为我出现乡村
——我是历史的地平线
母亲的黄昏和儿子的早晨

4

我属于船——
我属于船负重的毅力
但不属于它沉重的惰性

船诅咒我的任性
使它失去了宁静

我属于船——
我更属于纤夫的毅力
象皮鞭驱赶沉重的惰性

5

我累了，我想休息
想躺进纤夫平稳的鼾声

但大江又拍醒了征程
但启明又召来了晨曦
但峡谷又推出了小路
但露水又打湿了脚印

于是，纤夫和我一起
又拖起一个湿漉漉的早晨
……

宣　告

——给遇罗克烈士

北岛

也许最后的时刻到了
我没有留下遗嘱
只留下笔，给我的母亲
我并不是英雄
在没有英雄的年代里
我只想做一个人

宁静的地平线
分开了生者和死者的行列
我只能选择天空
绝不跪在地上
以显得刽子手们的高大
好阻挡那自由的风

从星星般的弹孔中
流出了血红的黎明

（选自《人民文学》1980年第10期）

履　历

北岛

我曾正步走过广场
剃光脑袋
为了更好地寻找太阳
却在疯狂的季节
转了向，隔着栅栏
会见那些表情冷漠的山羊
直到从盐碱地似的
白纸上看见理想
我弓起了脊背
自以为找到表达真理的
唯一方式，如同
烘烤着的鱼梦见海洋
万岁！我只他妈喊了一声
胡子就长出来
纠缠着，象无数个世纪
我不得不和历史作战
并用刀子与偶像们
结成亲眷，倒不是为了应付
那从蝇眼中分裂的世界
在争吵不休的书堆里
我们安然平分了
倒卖每一颗星星的小钱
一夜之间，我赌输了
腰带，又赤条条地回到世上
点着无声的烟卷
是给这午夜致命的一枪
当天地翻转过来
我被倒挂在
一棵墩布似的老树上
眺望

燧 石

高伐林

我是燧石
我棱角分明

我没有金钢石和祖母绿雍容华贵
也不如汉白玉或者翡翠典雅
我不曾雕成印玺　由诸侯拚命地争夺
也不配戴在摩登女郎的纤纤手指
或者在她们奶油般的脖子上悬挂
我更比不上漂移的冰川砾石
能成为地质论文里沉甸甸的砝码

我是燧石
我只有一个请求
请拾起我
——敲打

是的　狠狠地敲打!
一瞬间　真正的我挣开灰白的茧壳
从心灵深处　彩色的生命之光迸发

敲打吧　敲打会证明我
即使一万年沉睡在沼泽　山洼
也决不是　一粒废渣
而是一点凝固的火
一颗沉默的星
一朵坚硬的花
敲打吧　敲打会重现那一片往事
绚丽得象梦境中的朝霞
人类正是找到了我
才在荒芜中创造了文化
从楔形文字到金字塔
从彩陶　大乘佛教到徐悲鸿画马……

我是燧石
请记住我的体会吧
智慧之火　不是天外飞来
本来就埋在你的他的或她的脚下……

（选自《当代》1981年第4期）

誓 言

赵丽宏

凿在岩石上的
未必不朽
印成铅字的
未必永恒

云烟般飘过的
却不一定消失
流星般飞落的
却不一定流逝

一个真诚的微笑
一次心灵的顾盼
哪怕象无声的闪电
也远远胜过
雷鸣般虚张声势的
海誓山盟

1982年10月　上海

《星星》诗刊1983年3期

双桅船

舒婷

雾打湿了我的双翼
可风却不容我再迟疑
岸呵，心爱的岸
昨天刚刚和你告别
今天你又在这里
明天我们将在
另一个纬度相遇

是一场风暴，一盏灯
把我们联系在一起
是另一场风暴，另一盏灯
使我们再分东西
那怕天涯海角
岂在朝朝夕夕
你在我的航程上
我在你的视线里

旅馆之夜

舒婷

唇印和眼泪合作的爱情告示
勇敢地爬进邮筒
邮筒冰冷
久已不用
封条象绷带在风中微微摆动

楼檐在黑猫的爪下柔软起伏
大卡车把睡眠轧得又薄又硬
短跑选手
整夜梦见击发的枪声
魔术师接不住他的鸡蛋
路灯尖叫着爆炸
蛋黄的涂料让夜更加嶙峋

穿睡袍的女人
惊天动地拉开房门
光脚在地毯上狂奔如鹿
墙上掠过巨大的飞蛾
扑向电话铃声的蓬蓬之火

听筒里一片
沉寂
只有雪
在远方的电线上歌唱不息

1986年11月30日　福州

紫色的海星星

许德民

即使是威严的大海
也无力保护自己的孩子
在浩渺的波涛中
一个生命的失踪已不是新闻了
我看见游览区的小篮子里
海星星被标价出售
当奶白色的海月水母
伴随你巡视洁白的珊瑚林
你是骄傲的小女王
让淡紫色的光芒
　照耀着马蹄螺和虎斑贝
而我只用了几个小小的硬币
就换取了你
只是趴在我的手掌上
你柔软的肢体已变得僵硬

只有五个等边的触角
还是那样自信
自信而又哀伤
仿佛一遍一遍告诉我
你从来也没有伤害过谁
你怀念海洋里吹响蓝水泡的小伙伴
怀念不让小鲨鱼参加的
　捉迷藏的游戏

人间对你来说是陌生的
或许，你只是从沉船的残骸上
从少女飘沉的绣着并蒂莲
　　和蒲公英的丝手绢上
猜到了一些人间的秘密
但更多的仍然是一个迷
你一定开始后悔了
不该走出你的天国
　　那片洁白的珊瑚林

就连我也免不了后悔
不该用你凝固的眼泪
装饰我的小书桌
在我宁静的心里
竖起一座小小的墓碑
如果不知道世界上有你
心，大概不会这么沉重

并不是所有的善良
　　都能够得到应有的尊敬
并不是所有的伤害
　　都是蓄谋已久的
海星星啊
让我们成为朋友吧
我的心是你的珊瑚林

作品第39号

于坚

大街拥挤的年代
你一个人去了新疆
到开阔地去走走也好
在人群中你其貌不扬
牛仔裤到底牢不牢
现在可以试一试
穿了三年半　还很新
你可还记得那一回
我们讲得那么老实
人们却沉默不语
你从来也不嘲笑我的耳朵
其实你心里清楚
我们一辈子的奋斗
就是想装的象个人
面对某些美丽的女性
我们永远不知所措
不明白自己——究竟有多蠢
有一个女人来找过我
说你可惜了　凭你那嗓门
完全可以当一个男中音
有时想起你借过我的钱
我也会站在大门口
辨认那些乱糟糟的男子
我知道有一天你会回来
抱着三部中篇一瓶白酒
坐在那把四川藤椅上
演讲两个小时
仿佛全世界都在倾听
有时回头照照自己
心头一阵高兴
后来你不出声地望我一阵
夹着空酒瓶一个人回家

1983年

外科病房

王小龙

走廊上天竺葵也耷拉着脑袋
走来的都免不了垂头丧气
他们吃完晚饭把自己搬到床上
十分同情地凝视了一会儿雪白的绷带底下
那缺了一点什么的身体
然后故意把袖珍收音机开得哇啦哇啦响
想象自己假如是马拉多纳或者
是他妈的踢到门框上的足球
今天下午谁也没有来
那个每天下午给小伙子带来桔子和微笑的
　　姑娘
不会再来
那个小伙子昨天晚上乘大家睡着偷偷地死
　　了
早晨还有一只老麻雀跑来哭一阵
现在不知躲在哪个屋檐下琢磨一句诗
今天下午谁也没来
护士抱着自己一只脚象男人一样坐着
把信写得长长的没有最后一行
她一开灯天就黑了
天黑以后蚊子的嘴脸特别大
这个世界假如没有蚊子这个世界
无论如何不能算坏。

海边的孩子
——一本新诗集的序言

杨炼

我不知道那个孩子是谁
那个在海边做着快乐游戏的孩子
——沙土城堡和幻想的主人
　　草帽遮住眼睛
　　明朗地笑着
　　和太阳一同漫步
我不知道那个孩子是谁……

他那衣襟前别着蓝色的手帕
蓝蓝的，象写上生活全部奥秘的晴空
——他的脸就是一个美丽的梦
　　喃喃自语着
　　一个人来到这世界的海滨
　　为了与波涛谈话
我不知道那个孩子是谁……

我不知道那小篮子般的心里
是不是也盛着另外的回忆
——大海铺开淡淡的光芒
　　把笑声藏进永恒的谜语
　　可即使远处有暴风雨又怎样呢
　　世界依然是值得孩子们笑的
我不知道那个孩子是谁……

（选自《诗刊》1982年5期）

房间里的风景

杨炼

三十二岁　听够了谎言
再没有风景能够进这个房间
长着玉米面孔的客人
站在门口叫卖腐烂的石头
展览舌苔　一种牙缝里磨碎的永恒

他们或你都很冷　冷得想
被呕吐　象墙上亵渎的图画
记忆是一小队渐弱的地址
秋之芒草　死于一只金黄的赤足
谁凭窗听见星群消失
这一夜风声　仿佛掉下来的梨子
空房间被扔出去

在你赤裸的肉体中徘徊又徘徊
肢解　如天空和水
湿太阳　受伤吼叫时忘了一切
再没有风景能移入这片风景

直到最后一只鸟也逃往天上
在那手中碰撞　冻结成蓝色静脉
你把自己锁在那儿
这房间就固定在那儿　空旷的回声
背诵黑暗
埋葬你心里唯一的风景唯一的
　　谎言

日既出

马丽华

摇动十二万只风铃哗然而来
宇宙间饱和了恢宏和谐的回声
漫过草原一览无余的滩涂
太阳涨起大潮

阳光梳理我汹涌的思绪
思绪伸张为纷披的触须
沿着太阳的轨迹平行运转
在尽是矮个儿草墩的旷野
做一株挺拔的向日葵最适宜

不然谁又能变我为云朵呢
借殷勤的风之翼去接近他
是一座亘古挺立的山岩也好
风蚀为纷纷扬扬的大地微尘
承受他绵绵无尽的爱抚
不然谁能使我与爱之神同在

草叶曳动如经幡招摇
不为祈福专为祈爱
阳光下的生命只诵一字真言
我悄悄说，知道么
造物主为我创造了你
又因你而设计了我
唯我能够解破
　　　我与你的缘分之谜
我选择诗笔原只为太阳
　　　只为太阳你呀

激荡的草原忽然肃穆
体会最最新鲜最最深刻的感动
所有头颅都沉重地轻盈地扬起
朝同一方位致注目礼
隐隐传来赞美诗的和声
哦，从哪里响起，从哪个世纪响起

中国，我的钥匙丢了

梁小斌

中国，我的钥匙丢了。
那是十多年前，
我沿着红色大街疯狂地奔跑，
我跑到了郊外的荒野上欢叫，
后来，
我的钥匙丢了。

心灵，苦难的心灵
不愿再流浪了，
我想回家，
打开抽屉、翻一翻我儿童时代的画片，
还看一看那夹在书页里的
翠绿的三叶草。

而且，
我还想打开书橱，
取出一本《海涅歌谣》，
我要去约会，
我向她举起这本书，
做为我向蓝天发出的
爱情的信号。

这一切，
这美好的一切都无法办到，
中国，我的钥匙丢了。

天，又开始下雨，
我的钥匙啊，
你躺在哪里？
我想风雨腐蚀了你，
你已经锈迹斑斑了；
不，我不那样认为，
我要顽强地寻找，
希望能把你重新找到。

太阳啊，
你看见了我的钥匙了吗？
愿你的光芒
为它热烈地照耀。

我在这广大的田野上行走，
我沿着心灵的足迹寻找，
那一切丢失了的，
我都在认真思考。

1979年12月—1980年8月
（选自《诗刊》1980年第10期）

黑 夜

—— 在南行的火车上

王小妮

黑夜，
没有光亮。
无数只黑色的车轮，
颠簸在
近又看不见的地方。

伸出
所有的手指
所有的，
也摸不到
我所熟识的气息。

少了那双手，
连点燃了的火柴
都是黑色的。
只有，
这全黑的旅行包
和这里又漫长的
晚上。

我闭上眼睛，
用想象
去问候
那蓝色的房门。
一个好人的问候
能够穿透
全部黑夜，
使山川道路
都熠熠发光。

老祖父

李琦

雪花，在飞舞，
蓦地，我象又见到老祖父——
似乎是那样地清楚，
又是那样地模糊……

活着时，他是那么平凡，
佝偻着腰，
就如一棵掉尽叶子的老树……
下雪了，他便出去，
默默地，扫出一条路。
然后，象我欣赏着诗那样，
看着这条路上，
那来来往往的脚步……

今天，他走了，
静静地睡在大地深处。
雪飘飘，或许，
他的灵魂，
还在惦记着那神圣的义务？
啊，我出去了，
学他的样子，
去扫一条路……

石　壁

顾城

两块高大的石壁，
在倾斜中步步进逼。

是多么灼热的仇恨，
烧弯了铁黑的躯体。

树根的韧带紧紧绷住，
岩石的肌肉高高耸起，
可怕的角力就要爆发，
只要露水再落下一滴。

这一滴却在压缩中突然凝结，
时间变成了固体。
于是这古老的仇恨便得以保存，
引起了我今天一点惊异。

旗　帜

顾城

死亡是一个小小的手术
只切除了生命
甚至不留下伤口

手术后的人都异常平静
象一个岛屿睡在床上
风暴还没有过去
在白色的港口周围
聚集着捕鲸的船队

为了生活下去
人们创造了灵魂
创造了自由自在的帆
它们不受绳索的折磨
它们能在陆地上航行

黑色睡裙

唐亚平

我在深不可测的瓶子里灌满洗脚水
下雨的夜晚最有意味
约一个男人来吹牛
他到来之前我什么也没想
我放下紫色的窗帘开一盏发红的壁灯
黑睡裙在屋里荡了一圈
门已被敲响三次
他进门时带着一把黑伞
撑在屋子中间的地板上
我们开始喝浓茶
高贵的阿谀自来水一样哗哗流淌
甜蜜的谎言星星一样动人
我渐渐地随意地靠着沙发
以学者般的冷漠讲述老处女的故事
在我们之间上帝开始潜逃
捂着耳朵掉了一只拖鞋
在夜晚吹牛有种浑然的效果
在讲故事的时候
夜色越浓越好
雨越下越大越好

梦见苹果和鱼的安

何小竹

我仍然没有说
大房屋里就一定有死亡的蘑菇
你不断梦见苹果和鱼
就在这样的大房屋
你叫我害怕

屋后我写过的那黑森林
你从来就没去过
你总在重复那个梦境
你总在说
象真的一样

我们不会住很久了
我要把所有的门都加上锁
用草茎锁住鱼的嘴巴
一直到天亮
你还会在那个雨季
用毯子蒙住头
倾听大房屋
那些腐烂的声音吗

BIBLIOGRAPHY

Chinese Sources

Anthologies

Collected Poetry of Exploration 探索诗选. Edited by Jiang Jincheng 姜金城. Shanghai: Shanghai Literature and Arts Press, 1986.

Contemporary Chinese Experimental Poetry 中国当代实验诗选. Shenyang: Spring Wind Press, 1987.

Highlights of Chinese New Poetry: 1950–1980 中国新诗萃. Edited by Xie Mian 谢冕. Beijing: People's Literary Press, 1985.

Modern Chinese Love Poetry 中国现代爱情诗选. Edited by Wang Jiaxin 王家新. Wuhan: Yangtze Literary Press, 1981.

Selected Experimental Poetry 实验诗选. n.p., 1982.

Selected Lyrics of Contemporary China 中国当代抒情诗选. Edited by Yan Yi 雁翼. Guiyang: Guizhou People's Press, 1984.

Selected Modern Short Poetry 现代短诗选. Edited by Yan Yi 雁翼, Zhang Zhimin 张志民, and Li Na 李纳. Tianjin: Baihua Literary Press, 1984.

Selected Poems of 1979–1980 诗选. Chengdu: Sichuan People's Press, 1982.

Selected Poetry of 1981 一九八一年诗选. Beijing: People's Literary Press, 1983.

Selected Poetry of 1983 一九八三年诗选. Beijing: People's Literary Press, 1985.

Three Hundred Lyric Poems by Modern Young Poets 当代青年诗人抒情诗三百首. Edited by Huang Bangjun 黄邦军. Guiyang: Guizhou People's Press, 1985.

Women's Lyric Poetry 她们的抒情诗. Edited by Yan Chunde 阎纯德. Fuzhou: Fujian People's Press, 1983.

Individual Collections

Ai Qing 艾青. Edited by Gao Ying 高瑛. Hong Kong: Sanlian Press, 1982.
———. *Songs of the Return* 归来的歌. Chengdu: Sichuan People's Press, 1982.

Bei Dao 北岛. *Collected Poems* 北岛诗选. 2nd, expanded ed. Guangdong: New Century Publishing Co., 1987.

Cai Qijiao 蔡其矫. *The Double Rainbow* 双虹. n.p., 1981.
———. *The Drunken Stone* 醉石. Guangdong: Huacheng Press, 1986.
———. *Praying* 祈求. Jiangsu: Jiangsu People's Press, 1981.
———. *Songs of Life* 生活的歌. Beijing: People's Literary Press, 1982.

Liu Shahe 流沙河. *Collected Poems* 流沙河诗选. Shanghai: Literature and Arts Press, 1982.

Shao Yanxiang 邵燕祥. *In the Remote* 在远方. Guangdong: Huacheng Press, 1984.

Yan Yi 雁翼. *The Snow Welcomes Immigrating Wild Geese: Selected Poems* 雪迎征鸿, n.p., n.d.

————. *The Southern Tree* 南方的树. Guangdong: n.p., 1979.

General References

Barmé, Geremie, and John Minford, eds. *Seeds of Fire: Chinese Voices of Conscience.* New York: Hill and Wang, 1988.

Duke, Michael S. *Blooming and Contending: Chinese Literature in the Post-Mao Era.* Bloomington: Indiana University Press, 1985.

————, ed. *Contemporary Chinese Literature: An Anthology of Post-Mao Fiction and Poetry.* Armonk, N.Y. and London: M. E. Sharpe, 1985.

Goldblatt, Howard, ed. *Chinese Literature for the 1980s: The Fourth Congress of Writers and Artists.* Armonk, N.Y. and London: M. E. Sharpe, 1982.

Hsu, Kai-yu, ed. and trans. *Twentieth Century Chinese Poetry: An Anthology.* Ithaca: Cornell University Press, 1963.

Hsu, Kai-yu, and Ting Wang, eds. *Literature of the People's Republic of China.* Bloomington: Indiana University Press, 1980.

Lin, Julia C. *Modern Chinese Poetry: An Introduction.* Publications on Asia of the Institute for Comparative and Foreign Area Studies, no. 21. Seattle and London: University of Washington Press, 1972.

Link, Perry, ed. *Roses and Thorns: The Second Blooming of the Hundred Flowers in Chinese Fiction, 1979–80.* Berkeley: University of California Press, 1984.

————, ed. *Stubborn Weeds: Popular and Controversial Chinese Literature after the Cultural Revolution.* Bloomington: Indiana University Press, 1983.

Minford, John, ed. "Mists: New Poets from China." *Renditions: A Chinese-English Translation Magazine,* nos. 19–20 (Spring-Autumn, 1983): 181–270.

————. "Modernism and Tradition: A Symposium." *Renditions: A Chinese-English Translation Magazine,* nos. 19–20 (Spring-Autumn, 1983): 41–82.

Nieh, Hualing, ed. *Literature of the Hundred Flowers.* Vol. 2: *Poetry and Fiction.* New York: Columbia University Press, 1981.

Siu, Helen F., and Zelda Stern, eds. *Mao's Harvest: Voices from China's New Generation.* New York: Oxford University Press, 1983.